Supporting e-learning

Supporting e-learning
A guide for library and
information managers

Edited by
Maxine Melling

facet publishing

© This compilation: Maxine Melling 2005
The chapters: the contributors 2005

Published by
Facet Publishing
7 Ridgmount Street
London WC1E 7AE

Facet Publishing is wholly owned by CILIP: the Chartered Institute of Library
and Information Professionals.

First published 2005

British Library Cataloguing in Publication Data
A catalogue record for this book is available from the British Library.

ISBN 1-85604-535-8

Typeset from editor's disks by Facet Publishing in Elegant Garamond and
Humanist 521
Printed and made in Great Britain by MPG Books Ltd, Bodmin, Cornwall.

Contents

Contributors   vii

Introduction   xi
Maxine Melling

1   Managed learning environments: strategy, planning and
    implementation   1
    Sarah Porter

2   Process and partnerships   29
    Oleg Liber

3   Change management   55
    Robert Hunter, Stephen Clarke and Michele Shoebridge

4   Support in the use of new media   85
    Frank Moretti

5   Just one piece of the jigsaw: e-literacy in the wider perspective   113
    Peter Stubley

6   Collection management   139
    Frances Hall and Jill Lambert

    Index   165

Contributors

Stephen Clarke is the Head of e-learning at the University of Birmingham. He has been working with ICT in education since the late 1980s, first in secondary education and for the last eight years in higher education. He was responsible for introducing a campus-wide virtual learning environment to the University of Birmingham, a subject on which he has presented numerous conference papers. Before joining the University of Birmingham, Stephen worked in the medical school at the University of Oxford as an IT support manager; prior to that he was Head of Computer Science in a secondary school.

Frances Hall works as an information specialist (Engineering and Applied Science) at Aston University, liaising with five academic departments on the allocation of their library resource budgets. She is extensively involved in electronic resource selection, acquisition and promotion, and has been involved in the introduction of new services such as electronic books.

Robert Hunter is the founding Director of the Learning Development Unit at the University of Birmingham. He has over 20 years' experience of working in higher education of which the last 14 have involved development of systems and procedures to support the use of e-learning at an institutional level. Before joining the University of Birmingham Robert was Development Manager in the Centre for Access and Lifelong Learning at the University of Lincoln. There he worked with the Learning Support department and academic staff to develop a wide range of innovative e-learning projects, from setting up online systems and procedures to support the development of IT skills for students to the development and implementation of the University of Lincoln's own virtual campus, which was first used with over 2000 students in 1996.

Jill Lambert is the Team Leader for Science and Engineering and Head of Public Services in the Library and Information Services at Aston University. She has held professional posts in a range of organizations including the University of Central England, Staffordshire University, OCLC Europe, and the Universities of Northumbria and Westminster. She has published widely in the areas of subject support and collection management.

Oleg Liber is Professor of e-learning at Bolton Institute. He is also a director of the JISC Centre for Educational Interoperability Standards (CETIS) and project manager for the RELOAD project, developing standards-based tools for e-learning content and courses. He has been involved with learning technology for over 20 years, and has managed the development of a number of systems including the Colloquia Learning Environment. His research interests are primarily concerned with the use of organizational cybernetics in the education domain to inform the diagnosis and design of socio-technical systems for teaching and learning.

Maxine Melling is Director of Learning and Information Services at Liverpool John Moores University, where she is responsible for the management of a converged library and computer support service. Her professional background is in further and higher education library services and, in addition to strategic management, has included responsibility for areas such as information literacy, staff training and development, and quality management systems. Her wider professional activities include active involvement in cross-sectoral library collaboration. She has published on a number of topics including customer service and quality management systems.

Frank Moretti is co-founder of the Columbia Center for New Media Teaching and Learning (CCNMTL) for which he provides pedagogical, strategic and managerial leadership. In addition to defining the goals and disseminating the CCNMTL message on campus, Frank acts as the pedagogical leader and has recently received recommendation for funding in NSF's Teacher Professional Continuum (TPC) programme for Video Interactions for Teaching and Learning (VITAL): a Learning Environment for Courses in Early Mathematics Education. He has been the Executive Producer of numerous interactive learning environments, one of which, Brownfield Action, recently won the SENCER Award for one of the four best undergraduate curricula in science. Frank serves as Professor of Communications, Computing and Technology at Teachers College. Prior to joining Teachers College, Frank served as the Associate Headmaster at the Dalton School, where he was also Executive Director of their New Laboratory for Teaching and Learning, which he co-founded in 1989, and of the internationally known Dalton Technology Plan. Frank is recognized as one of America's leading theorists and practitioners in the use of digital technology in education. Before Dalton, Frank served at New York University as Director of the General Studies Program, the two year college, and the BA Program for Adults.

Sarah Porter is the Head of Development at the Joint Information Systems Committee (JISC). Sarah has responsibility for the development strategy for the JISC and its implementation through more than 200 development projects, many of which are building technologies for learning, teaching and research based on standards and specifications. Sarah has particular interest in using technology to support learning and teaching, and leads a number of programmes in this area. Currently these include investigating e-learning and pedagogy, the sharing and re-using of learning objects through repositories and portals, technical frameworks for e-learning and a £13 million programme to explore distributed e-learning.

Michele Shoebridge is currently Director of Information Services at the University of Birmingham. Michele has been involved, and very proactive, for many years with learning and teaching activities at the University of Birmingham. She is a member of the Board of CURL (the Consortium of University and Research Libraries), Chair of the CURL Steering Group on Monograph InterLending, Member of the Resource Discovery Network Board and Convenor of the Universitas 21 Information Service Group. Michele is an institutional representative on SCONUL (Society of College, National and University Libraries), RUGIT (Russell Group IT Directors) and the West Midlands Higher Education Association Libraries Group.

Peter Stubley is Assistant Director for Academic Services at the University of Sheffield Library, with responsibility for the management of library support to academic departments for learning and teaching, and research. In this role, he is taking a fresh look at the way in which the library needs to be organized to support new methods of learning and teaching, particularly via the introduction of virtual learning environments and related new technologies. Apart from this work, his interests are library building design and research into multimedia applications and the use of Z39.50; he was Project Director for the eLib-funded RIDING clumps project and led the Feasibility Study into a National Union Catalogue for the UK in 2000–1.

Introduction

Maxine Melling

Definitions and terminology

Some writers have already expressed dismay at the proliferation of 'e-terminology', with one reviewer (Paschoud, 2003) ironically calling for a new movement which refers to any academic or administrative process that involves a piece of paper being prefixed with the letter p ('p-learning, p-government' and so on). Admittedly the language of e-learning can be very clumsy and a proper understanding can be hampered by inconsistent use of terminology as the exponential rate of change prevents us from catching up with agreed definitions. However, arguing over definitions can become a very happy displacement activity. With that in mind one definition of e-learning, borrowed from the LTSN Generic Centre (Jenkins and Hanson, 2003), is offered here and it is hoped that this will suffice: 'Learning facilitated and supported through the use of information and communication technologies'. As such, this volume allows that e-learning might encompass the use of electronic content, virtual learning environments, managed learning environments and all variations in between.

Background

This collection of essays aims to address some of the strategic and operational issues that library and information services (LIS) managers might consider in supporting e-learning. The authors who have contributed to it bring very personal perspectives, influenced by experience of supporting e-learning in their own institutions. It is fair to say that the full potential of e-learning has yet to be realized in further and higher education. Educational institutions are in the process of developing e-strategies and in working out what changes are likely to occur as these strategies are put into practice. Library and information services reflect this relative instability. Although significant developments have already taken place, we don't yet know what the full impact of e-learning will be on our services or on the role played by library and information staff in colleges and universities. Some practitioners are working on the practical application of new technologies. Some are concentrating on the changes that are taking place to existing service models. Others are starting to conceptualize new models. The authors who have contributed to this volume reflect this diversity of approach. However, it is clear that they have a shared understanding of some common themes which underpin the successful support of e-learning. These themes are considered in brief below and are examined in more detail in the chapters that follow.

The diversity of approach reflected in these essays emphasizes that there can be no off-the-shelf model for the development and support of e-learning. The need for locally based approaches is further emphasized when considering the differing aspirations of many educational institutions in relation to the development of e-learning. It isn't unusual for academic institutions to view e-learning as the enabling route to ambitious aspirations such as increased participation, cost reduction and improved diversity. These can seem modest, however, when compared with a recent UK Government statement (DfES, 2003) which claims that e-learning can 'contribute to all the Government's objectives for education – to raising standards, improving quality; removing barriers to learning and participation in learning; preparing for employment; up-skilling the workplace; and ultimately, ensuring that every learner achieves their full potential'. It may be that your organization is seeking to address all these challenges at once, but it is more likely that e-learning is contextualized in a more focused and locally relevant mission within which LIS needs to agree its own contribution.

Local structures also determine the role taken by LIS in supporting e-learning. In 2002 a straw poll survey of UK university library and information services (Melling, 2002) was carried out to discover if there was any common institutional ownership and responsibility for emerging web-based learning support. The responses showed an almost equal split of organizational responsibility between educational technology departments, computing departments and libraries, with some faculty ownership in universities organized on a collegiate basis. Consultation with the survey respondents made it apparent that the determining factors for an institution's choice of approach tended to be the result of local organizational structures and culture, with some notable exceptions being the result of the strength of character or reputation of the director of the responsible department. Although anecdotal, this evidence is backed up by subsequent studies. For example, membership of a recent OCLC e-learning Task Force (OCLC, 2003a) reflected a diverse and complex range of approaches to e-learning, which highlighted that there could be no 'one-size-fits-all approach in terms of solutions to interactions between libraries and e-learning environments'.

Although significant developments have taken place in relation to technological support and increased access to electronic content, we have hardly started to address relevant questions in relation to the fundamental cultural changes that are required. One of the most interesting and challenging aspects of e-learning is the emergence of new and complex links between aspects of learning and learning support that have previously been able to exist in isolation, or at least to operate only in parallel with one another. The OCLC Task Force members (OCLC, 2003a) identified the main areas of interdependency as pedagogy, learning methodologies and technology, arguing that a better understanding and assessment of the links between the three is an essential priority. The creation of effective links between these areas affects a range of issues of importance to those responsible for delivery of learning and information support, not least how staff within service teams and teaching departments work together.

Effective e-learning is dependent upon a different model of collaboration. It isn't unreasonable to suggest that the different academic stakeholder groups are often culturally and organizationally quite separate. The terminology used by them can be dissimilar, as can the service culture that they take for granted. What is required for the effective support of learners in an electronic environment is a new service convergence which has less to do with structural organization and more to do with the adoption of common terminology and approaches to support. As emphasized by a number of contributors to this volume of essays, e-learning requires a process-based approach to support in preference to one which is contained within structural boundaries. A recent information landscape study (OCLC, 2003b) argued that 'creating, managing and delivering content in an e-learning environment requires the conscious and planned collaboration of several sectors of a university's community. Faculty, IT staff, administrative staff and librarians all have roles and responsibilities in content management; however, these sectors have generally worked relatively autonomously from one another. Co-operation and collaboration become crucial.' Users of electronic learning environments are increasingly unaware of the identity of the department or individual responsible for whatever lies behind the portal they are using. The protection of organizational barriers is therefore likely to add confusion.

While risking the danger of pushing an argument just too far, the requirement for collaboration can also be applied to digital content, either in terms of the re-use of learning objects or in relation to shared ownership and responsibility. In a digital environment the question of ownership becomes very blurred. Libraries are providing access to digital material that they may only be leasing from a provider. Increasingly, libraries are also creating metadata and access routes to learning objects created by academic colleagues. Similarly, teaching staff may be using learning objects created by colleagues in different subject disciplines.

Consultation on the Higher Education Funding Council's draft e-Learning Strategy (Glenaffric Ltd, 2004) identified what respondents saw as a lack of emphasis on learner support. In particular 'respondents felt that the e-learning strategy should include more emphasis on developing appropriate learner support and guidance (specifically including non-teaching staff) and the central role of libraries and information services in learning'. The links and inter-relationships that are central to e-learning place a requirement on learner support that goes beyond the passive delivery of content and services and points to a more proactive service model. In many ways one of the most interesting changes that has started to emerge from support in a digital environment is the emphasis on learning outcomes and therefore on the impact of the support services available from LIS. An understanding of this service model is still being conceptualized and is addressed by several of the contributors to this volume of essays.

It has been said that library and information services are struggling to find a clear role for themselves in the e-learning environment. Indeed, the OCLC Environmental Scan (Glenaffric Ltd, 2004) argued that '[e-learning] is a growing and dynamic environment, one in which fluidity and change are the norm culturally, institutionally and technically. Within this environment the academic library is still searching for a permanent, comfortable and serviceable position that is nimble enough to be flexible, accessible and continually up-to-date within a wider university structure.' There can be little doubt that support for e-learning requires flexibility and creativity. The essays contained in this volume offer the reader some alternatives to such an approach.

The chapters

In Chapter 1 Sarah Porter contextualizes e-learning within the broader framework of the development of managed learning environments (MLEs). MLEs are described in this chapter as part of a growing trend, in the UK academic sector, to plan integrated systems that support learning, teaching and research across all departments. The theme of integration and inter-relationships is one that occurs throughout this volume of essays. Sarah Porter's argument is that LIS departments need to understand these links and, most importantly, need to be self-determining in relation to their own institutional role; taking cognizance of the local drivers for developing an e-strategy. In common with other contributors Sarah Porter highlights the need to know where you're going before you decide how to get there. It's worth making this rather obvious statement at the beginning of a volume that considers e-learning. Because of the rapid growth and sophistication of the technology there's a real danger in letting this become the driving force, rather than in agreeing learning and teaching goals and then considering how the technology can help achieve them.

Sarah Porter points to the ubiquity of MLE development in UK universities and colleges, with a recorded 70% of institutions having already developed a MLE. Institutions are using MLEs to provide a single point of access to information and to streamline administration, as well as to support and encourage e-learning. For those still considering how best to embark on the development of a managed learning environment, Sarah Porter provides a step-by-step guide to the process, highlighting issues such as the identification of key stakeholders, the definition of strategic objectives and the access links required to e-learning resources.

In Chapter 2 Professor Oleg Liber considers the changes brought about in academic institutions by the use of new technologies and considers how these changes impact on organizational structures and partnerships. In charting the evolution of learning technologies Professor Liber notes the importance of the mainstreaming of integrated systems and the growing pressure on service teams to develop a more proactive role, particularly as web-based applications become the norm. He sees an inevitable move towards LIS staff working more flexibly with teaching colleagues, with this development leading to changes in traditional service models. Professor Liber highlights the need for LIS staff to develop relevant pedagogic and technical skills.

What is particularly important in such a fast-changing environment is the ability of organizational structures to exist in a constant state of flux, with academic institutions being flexible enough to adopt new processes as changes occur to the existing ones.

Professor Liber stresses that different academic subject departments may need different e-learning solutions and also need to be able to experiment and make mistakes in a supportive environment. One of the roles of service departments, therefore, is to negotiate technological solutions within this context. In stressing the need for service teams to put themselves in the position of the teacher and to focus on the outcomes required of any e-learning support solution, Professor Liber introduces a theme which is picked up time and time again by other contributors to this volume and which emphasizes a move from passive service delivery to a more proactive involvement with the learning process. In order to manage the process of change Professor Liber offers a common methodology (TASCOE), which assists departments in clarifying existing institutional processes and in determining the most appropriate role to help them to work within these processes.

Changing roles and responsibilities are also emphasized by Robert Hunter, Stephen Clarke and Michele Shoebridge, who in Chapter 3 offer an approach for the development of an e-learning strategy. In common with other contributors they also emphasize the importance of looking beyond what the technology can achieve and focusing on the required learning outcomes.

In this chapter the authors recommend the change management toolkit developed by the UK Chartered Institute of Library and Information Professionals (CILIP). The toolkit enables organizations to analyse the environment and to develop locally relevant support structures. Having described this process the chapter's authors provide a step-by-step guide to the development and implementation of an e-learning strategy, stressing the importance of embedding e-learning into staffing structures and work-flow processes. The authors repeat Oleg Liber's emphasis on the importance of developing LIS staff skills and of ensuring that staff are active participants in the learning process.

In Chapter 4 the change management processes considered in the first three chapters are reflected and linked more directly to practice in Professor Frank Moretti's description of the driving principles behind the work of Columbia University's Center for New Media Teaching and Learning. Professor Moretti provides a robust critique of existing service models that are based within an established environment with predictable and routine calls upon them. In agreement with Oleg Liber, Professor Moretti argues that the nature of digital technology requires a more flexible and proactive service model, which moves away from a passive conservatism to a proactive creativity.

Professor Moretti believes that access to information has become seen as the same thing as learning, the web's vast pool of information having become a substitute for purposeful activity in a constructed environment. One of his main arguments is that e-learning support teams need to add a layer of services between the information and the learner. Rather than simply and passively providing e-resources librarians must also suggest tools and contexts within which learning can take place. This approach places a requirement on the architects of digital libraries and the pedagogues to work together. Professor Moretti goes on to provide very practical case studies, based on the work of his team of staff at Columbia University, of how this approach can be developed successfully. He stresses that support teams need to ask how they can add value to the learning experience.

The chapter concludes with a list of guidelines for best practice which should, arguably, be mandatory reading for all technical support teams. These include admonitions to avoid being blinded by a love of technology into providing over-complex solutions, to be honest about the time needed to introduce e-learning support systems, and to listen to what the teachers say they are trying to achieve – the learning outcomes – before leaping in with a technical solution.

Professor Moretti's theme of active collaboration between support teams and academics is continued and illustrated in Chapter 5 by Peter Stubley, in his consideration of how best to embed e-literacy into the curriculum and into student life. He places his discussion of e-literacy in the context of the social and political changes that have taken place in UK higher education as well as a broader consideration of students' skills needs. He also provides an analysis of the relationship between library staff and academics in the area of information skills training, which is likely to strike a chord with many readers not least in its exploration of the tensions that often exist between the librarian's belief that information literacy is self-evidently a 'good thing' and the academic's seeming inability to be overwhelmed by this. In exploring these issues Peter Stubley, in common with previous authors, places responsibility upon LIS staff to engage in an improved dialogue with academic colleagues, illustrating how this might be done by describing a collaborative model for the integration of e-literacy into the virtual learning environment that is used at the University of Sheffield.

Peter Stubley provides very practical examples of how an electronic environment might allow new and innovative approaches to traditional problems. For example, the University of Sheffield has been able to re-think its approach to managing reading lists by using the functionality of the VLE and other software applications to link the re-named 'resource list' to both digital objects and to circulation details. He also describes how the Library is focusing on the potential afforded by the creation of information skills learning objects in order to embed e-literacy course content across all University departments.

A number of the contributors to this volume advocate a more proactive working relationship between academic and support services in the delivery of effective e-learning support. Peter Stubley describes how the University of Sheffield has attempted to manage such an approach, using forums, meetings and away days to generate enthusiasm and facilitate discussion. He also advocates the need to consider the re-organization of library teams in order to better facilitate what Sheffield has called 'new partnerships'.

In Chapter 6 Frances Hall and Jill Lambert continue to look at the very practical impact of e-learning by considering collection management, and specifically the provision and exploitation of electronic resources. They offer approaches to the selection of e-resources and their integration within a virtual learning environment, as well as providing advice on issues such as authentication and promotion.

Hall and Lambert link to the previous chapter by describing how an awareness of electronic resources is becoming an established component of information literacy programmes, describing recent initiatives to embed web-based information skills within a virtual learning environment. The chapter provides a number of useful links to current initiatives, including those associated with the development of institutional repositories and with the creation of common standards to enable interoperability.

References

Glenaffric Ltd (2004) *Responses to Consultations on the HEFCE E-learning Strategy, a report to HEFCE by Glenaffric Ltd, May 2004*, www.hefce.ac.uk/pubs/rdreports/2004/rd04_04/rd_04_04.doc.

Great Britain. Department for Education and Skills (2003) *Towards a Unified E-learning Strategy, Consultation Document*, London, DfES.

Jenkins, M. and Hanson, J. (2003) *A Guide for Senior Managers*, E-Learning Series 1, LTSN Generic Centre.

Melling, M. (2002) An unpublished survey by lis-sconul.

Online Computer Library Center (2003a) *Libraries and the Enhancement of E-learning*, Dublin OH, OCLC, www5.oclc.org/downloads/community/elearning.pdf.

Online Computer LIbrary Center (2003b) *Environmental Scan: a report to the OCLC membership*, Dublin OH, OCLC, www.oclc.org/membership/escan/tic.htm.

Paschoud, J. (2003) *E-learning and Teaching in Library and Information Services, [by B. Allan, Facet Publishing]* a book review, www.ariadne.ac.uk/issue34/paschoud/intro.html.

1

Managed learning environments: strategy, planning and implementation

Sarah Porter

Introduction

The concept of the managed learning environment (MLE) may not seem to be of essential interest or concern to library and information services (LIS). It can seem that the MLE is of more relevance to IT departments and those who maintain the institutional virtual learning environment (VLE) or learning management system such as Blackboard, WebCT or LearnWise. However, the essential aspect of the MLE is that it has the potential to include any and all systems and processes that support learning and teaching. As most LIS support learning and teaching activity, a MLE is relevant to the core functions of LIS. The term MLE describes a growing trend to plan integrated systems that support learning and teaching across all departments or functions within an educational organization – from the registry to the academic departments to the library. If the college or university is developing a MLE, then the library and information services should be part of the planning group. In some cases, library and information services may be best placed to lead the process of MLE development.

Each information service needs to decide what role it wants to play in supporting learning and teaching through technology. The aim of this chapter is to help you decide what that role should be. The chapter provides an overview of the MLE concept; briefly describes the MLE development process; discusses those aspects of the MLE that are most relevant to library and information services; and gives some examples of MLE models.

Definitions

The Joint Information Systems Committee (JISC) definition of a MLE is: 'the whole range of information systems and processes of a college or university (including its VLE if it has one) that contribute directly, or indirectly, to learning and the management of that learning'.

To articulate this more clearly, the MLE requires both a *strategic* approach and a *systems* approach. Without strategy, the MLE will not be appropriate or sustainable; without planned systems, there will be no MLE. (This has implications for technical and 'soft' systems, such as offline processes, training, support and change management. Some of these issues will be covered in more depth in other chapters.)

So, another definition of a MLE might be: strategic planning of organizational e-systems to support learning and teaching.

Why do we need MLEs?

We have all seen a vast increase in the availability and use of computerized systems in recent years. As recently as the 1980s there were few users of computer systems, and limited applications and data for users to access. Activity was mainly focused on specialist applications for particular disciplines, such as the Minitab statistics package used for social science research. Supercomputers processed large quantities of data, for instance analysing substantial banks of textual data and querying databases, but these were generally programmed and managed by experts rather than 'users'. The information world was comparatively advanced in its use of computers as many computerized library catalogues were put in place in the early 1980s. However, these were not generally used by academic staff and certainly not by students; but by 2002 54% of households in the UK owned a personal computer (PC). This represents a substantial rise in computer ownership from 1985 when only 13% of the population owned one (Office of National Statistics, 2004).

In 2005 we are in a completely different 'Brave New World'. Technological goods and services are even cheaper and more widely available, and more and more people have access to reasonably priced desktop computers. As a result, these computers are now considered to be the norm and to be required: we expect every teacher and every student at a university or college to have access to a computer, and that computer should be connected to the internet.

The information revolution

At the same time as far more people have been gaining access to computers, there has been a massive increase in the amount of information that is available to us in computer-readable formats. First came electronic publishing, where increasing numbers of resources were made available in both hard-copy and digital format, and some as 'born digital' resources. Publishers experimented with the new capabilities of the digital medium by developing multimedia and interactive resources. The second wave has threatened at times to swamp us: the internet has made available an unimaginable range and quantity of digital resources at low or no cost, but with little quality assurance.

In parallel, almost every human endeavour now spawns a computerized system, and education is not excluded from this. So the university administrative function owns huge student information systems, payroll systems, estates management and so on. The teaching departments often have their own student management systems, course databases and teaching materials held in a virtual learning environment or similar system (Currier, Brown and Ekmekioglu, 2001).

In most universities and colleges there are many different sources of information and many different access points to that information (Dolphin and Sherratt, 2003). This would not be a problem in an environment where individuals played a single role and accessed a finite number of systems; but it is a problem within a university where a member of staff needs to cross over all of those 'silos' and access library resources, research data, contribute to teaching resources, book teaching rooms and also be paid on time! Our university e-systems have developed organically, hence, in many cases, we have a mass of competing and contradictory systems. For example, as part of the work of the INSIDE project, St Andrew's University found that there were at least 50 databases that might be included within their MLE (Allison, 2003).

How do MLEs help to achieve strategy?

The concept of managed learning environments first emerged from the further education sector where national committees wanted to encourage colleges to embrace the potential of new technologies, but realized that this needed to be clearly planned and focused upon the main business of colleges: the learning and teaching activity. The MLE diagram developed by Becta (see Figure 1.1, page 6) encapsulated the message that learning activity needed to form the focus for all relevant institutional systems and processes, and that integration of systems might be needed to support learning activities properly.

Over the last three years the MLE concept has generated high levels of interest in the UK higher education community. The resonance has been particularly strong as many universities have adopted large-scale implementations of learning management systems or VLEs and these systems are presenting many challenges to the status quo. Large-scale use of VLEs requires teaching departments, IT services, libraries and administration to work together in a way that they never have done before.

The JISC carried out a survey of MLE development in 2003. Its detailed analysis was based upon a 15-page questionnaire that was completed by over 50% of UK higher education institutions (HEIs), as well as some further education colleges and a number of more detailed case studies. The survey found that over 70% of organizations are developing a MLE and the main driver for development is 'Enhancing the quality of teaching and learning'. The report, however, notes that most developments to date have focused upon the enhancement of the student 'experience' rather than the learning – that is, they have provided easier, more convenient access to information, resources and tools, but not noticeably (or measurably) affected learning (Education for Change, 2003).

The report also identified a number of additional factors that are driving MLE development, reporting variance across institutions. The survey data reflects the common interests and concerns of universities today. Frequently cited factors for MLE development include:

- improving access to learning for students off-campus
- widening participation, inclusiveness
- student expectations
- improving access to learning for part-time students
- using technology to deliver e-learning
- having a committed local 'champion'
- to help standardizing across institution
- competitive advantage
- improved administrative processes
- attracting new markets
- attracting home students.

In conclusion, we can see that for some institutions the move towards an e-systems strategy is driven by local concerns such as widening participation. For others, it may stem from an intention to re-develop all processes to be more efficient and IT-aware: to develop a 'digital university'. Both drivers for development can be accommodated by the right MLE design. However, it is important that the main driver is recognized from the start so that success can be measured. Each driver for the development of a MLE will have different implications for library and information services. Different MLE models will be considered in a later section.

What do MLEs look like?

The three essential perspectives of a MLE are the user, organizational and technical views. It is likely that the MLE will have a number of different user interfaces. From a user perspective, many MLEs to date have focused on making available data from a number of different sources, such as student information systems and module catalogues, through a single interface. This interface may be aimed at a particular user or group of users. An administrator may view payroll data from the MLE while an academic may view departmental minutes and their payroll details. Typically, the user can log into the portal and it will 'personalize' some of the information that is provided. For example, students at the University of Plymouth log into a web page and can access their e-mail, calendar, learning resources and so on from a single web page (Bouch and Wilks, 2002).

From a technical perspective the MLE may appear as a collection of servers, databases, applications and software, which are connected together in some way. In some instances the level of technical integration may be quite low. The use of 'thin' portal technology will allow the user to see a single view of the systems without those systems being connected – each system may be joined separately to the portal software. In most cases, some level of integration or data-sharing is in place, such as the transfer of data about individual students into other systems. Figure 1.1 shows a technical view of a MLE.

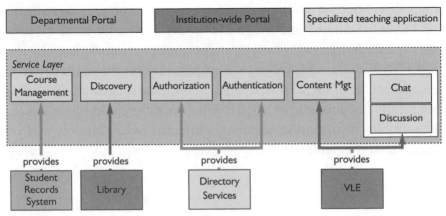

Figure 1.1   A technical view of a MLE (JISC, 2003)

Architectures for MLEs

A MLE is not a single technical system and is specific to an institution and its particular requirements. This is because it usually needs to integrate with existing systems and processes and because it may include a range of different systems depending on the strategic objectives. For example, one university may choose to include all of its administrative systems within the staff view of the MLE, while a smaller university may decide to focus only on the integration of student data systems.

Thus it follows that there is no single technical architecture for a MLE and, despite what some commercial suppliers claim, there is no single model that should be adopted to integrate systems. In order to design an appropriate architecture for a MLE, a university or college will need to review its current systems' architectures against user requirements for a new system.

There is growing international interest in the use of service-oriented architectures and web services to share data between disparate systems – across internal or external networks and the internet, using standard protocols. The use of web services fits well with the concept of MLEs as web services can be used to move data between any number of different systems, providing that appropriate interfaces have been developed. It is useful to be aware of this growing trend as it may influence choices that you make about technologies.

There may be several different organizational perspectives to a MLE but there must be a strategic overview of the MLE, with a clear understanding of what it aims to achieve, for whom and to what timescales. Usually there will be a description of information stores, flows and processes within the MLE, such as how student record data is captured through registration processes and then fed on to other systems. Depending upon the level of co-dependence between systems and the number of aspects of the MLE that are being integrated, this information mapping may range from simple to highly complex.

Some typical MLE models

As discussed above, different types of MLE may be developed depending on the key strategic drivers for the development and who is driving development forward. In some cases, the library or information services may wish to supply content to the MLE, such as information about short-loan resources that are relevant to a particular module. In other cases, it may make sense for the library to act as a recipient of information, such as student record data. You will want to consider both aspects of this when considering how the library systems might integrate within a MLE.

Scenario 1: MLE to support e-learning

In one scenario the priority of MLE development may be to support learners using e-learning technologies. In some cases the development will focus upon a particular group of users, for example distance learning students. In others it will include local students who receive a mixture of face-to-face teaching and e-learning and distance learners. In both cases, technology is used in an attempt to provide access to the same level of service that can be accessed on campus. Sometimes e-learning applications will provide additional opportunities for learners such as multimedia, greater opportunities for discussion and collaborative work, and specialized access such as to virtual laboratories.

In all situations, the learner will need to access a wide range of different information and online resources. Some of these will be created by teaching departments or specialist units; others will (or should) be accessed from within LIS holdings. Perhaps the biggest challenge for us in providing a coherent online learning experience is deciding to what extent we should integrate learning resources 'seamlessly' into an e-learning environment, and to what extent we should expect learners to develop information skills to locate resources for themselves. Whatever decisions are made, LIS will have a very important role to play in this scenario, as discussed below.

Scenario 2: MLE for integrated user support (staff and students)

Some MLE systems are designed to meet the needs of a large range of users across a large range of functions. The strategy for some MLE developments is to provide a single point of access for all information sources that might be used by staff or students. In this case, the design of the MLE needs to focus on the user and be based on their requirements, rather than based on the current systems that are in place. As well as back-end data sharing and single authentication, a portal may be used to bring together services into a single web page for the learner to make it easy for them to locate and use services.

In a large and complex organization with many legacy systems this can be challenging – development will need to be planned to take place incrementally with regular review points, to ensure that the whole development is not threatened by problems with one or more systems. Where a large-scale MLE is planned, the benefits to users need to be clear: there is no point carrying out integration for its own sake. Will it really make a difference to a student if they can't update their home address online – or could they just as easily do this by telephone, as they do at present? If the cost of developing this function runs into thousands of pounds, the implementation may not be justifiable.

Scenario 3: MLE for streamlined administration

With this scenario the main strategic aim is to reduce the administrative burden on staff (teaching and support or administration) by providing an integrated source of accurate data about students. In this case, the MLE may provide a limited range of functions to the user, but draw upon a large amount of secure data that is owned by the administrative departments. This may be complex to implement and require careful negotiations. There may be potential for LIS to benefit from this type of scenario by making use of the user data that is being collated by other departments. LIS may also wish to consider whether any of their administrative processes can be aligned with those of other departments to make data collection more efficient, and to simplify the user experience. For example, payment for library fines might be managed through the same interface as payment for tuition fees.

First steps towards developing a MLE

The following section describes some of the first steps to take when developing a MLE. Readers are referred to JISC's *Creating an MLE* infokit, which is freely available on the web, for a detailed and comprehensive guide to MLE development. It includes step-by-step guides to each step towards development, links to examples and case studies, and information about evaluation (JISC, 2003).

Step 1: identify stakeholders

One of the crucial issues about MLE development is that responsibility for its design and implementation will necessarily cross many institutional boundaries. Even where a university that is introducing a MLE has integrated information and learning services, academic departments will be managed separately, and even within a converged service there are often silos of information ownership and management. The MLE needs to be developed with the participation of key stakeholders and with consideration of current activities with which the MLE needs to align, such as the procurement of a new student information system or the development of an e-learning strategy. The range of stakeholders that should be involved in the MLE development may be wider than first expected.

In general, the key groups to be involved in MLE development (or where development may already be underway) are:

- IT services
- library services
- administrative departments, such as the registry
- student services

- teaching departments
- learning and teaching support unit.

The MLE development may be led by one group or, more typically, by a cross-departmental working group or committee that plans the development together. If you intend to initiate MLE activities, it is advisable to work through existing strategic cross-departmental groups where they exist, and to ensure that all relevant stakeholders are invited to be involved in any new group. Political goodwill and support from the right strategic decision-makers are crucial to achieving success in this type of long-term and potentially costly venture.

Step 2: define strategic objectives for the MLE

This move towards the adoption of e-learning technologies across the board provides the impetus for change. However, well articulated strategy is needed to make that change successful. What are we trying to achieve? What do we need to change and what do we need to preserve? Is our change to be incremental, iterative or at one time? A vision for the future that is shared between the relevant institutional functions can provide the roadmap to success.

To create a managed learning environment within an organization one needs to be clear on the strategic objectives and then design the systems that will best achieve them. The MLE or e-systems strategy should relate closely to existing institutional strategies such as the learning and teaching strategy, e-learning strategy or information strategy. The MLE strategy must support these existing strategies and illustrate how it does so – rather than appearing to be an additional 'bolt-on' or burden. Discrete projects (such as the implementation of a new library system) work well over a finite timescale; however, changes that will have an impact on many existing systems and processes require strategic-level support across a longer lifecycle. Thus a strategy is needed that clearly supports the relevant institutional objectives: 'for effective and efficient linkage of VLEs/MLEs and digital and hybrid libraries, senior university management must support from above with long term strategic planning, identifying their own specific cultural, social and educational requirements' (Currier, Brown and Ekmekioglu, 2001).

JISC's *Creating an MLE* provides other useful guidelines and resources to aid the development of a MLE strategy; it is a useful reference point to ensure that all the main issues have been considered at the planning stage. See Figure 1.2.

You should aim to provide a brief summary of the scale, scope and intended outcomes. For example are you intending to totally integrate all your systems (finance, student records, VLE, timetabling, web sites, etc) or are you focusing in on specific aspects (linking your VLE with your student record system or integrating systems concerned with teaching and assessment)? Consider the following:

- What is the scope of the work and what will it broadly involve?
- How did the idea come about?
- What are the main reasons for doing it?
- Who is going to lead it?
- Who else will be involved?
- Who are the stakeholders?
- What are the potential organisational benefits?
- Are there any barriers which might effect your MLE development?
- What are the timescales for developing and implementing your MLE?
- What are the intended outcomes of the project?
- Where can you get additional advice, support or guidelines?

Figure 1.2   Questions to consider when developing a MLE (JISC, 2003)

These questions need to be addressed by a group that should include the main stakeholders for the development of learning and teaching support systems. It may be possible to begin this analysis within a single department and to bring others into discussions at a later stage, but it is important to achieve buy-in by all the key parties to the intended outcomes and the processes by which the outcomes will be achieved .

Step 3: MLE design

Once the decision to develop a MLE has been made, you need to create a design for the systems that fits the scope of your objectives. It is likely that the system design will need to be iterative – reviewed regularly and changed as required.

> All elements of MLE development are linked together and a successful design is a product of successful implementation of all the other stages both before and after. It is more useful to think of your project in layers that interact rather than solely in stages. The design process itself needs to be constantly in a state of change. The design of a MLE needs to reflect the user needs, and institutions never stand still. (JISC, 2003)

The MLE design should be created and owned by the manager of the MLE implementation project. It is important that information specialists contribute to the design at all stages to ensure that information needs are considered.

As described above, the MLE design needs to have three aspects: technical, organizational and user-focused. Each aspect will have its own set of documentation, which articulates an understanding of the current situation and the plans for the future.

The technical design may include systems diagrams that explain how technical systems will be integrated, how data be will transferred, and so on. The organizational aspect will explain issues such as ownership of data within the system, processes for back-up and archiving of data. The user view will include explanations of how the system can be used, test versions of the system, user documentation and user requirements.

By the end of the MLE design process you will have a substantial body of material that describes the strategy for the MLE, its technical architecture and the organizational structures that will be affected by its implementation. Note that all three aspects of the design must be revisited and updated as internal and external factors change. Internal factors, such as responding to user feedback, may need to be taken into account in a re-design but so may unforeseen, external factors, such as the procurement of a new administrative system by some of the teaching departments.

To plan the MLE, identify the stakeholders who will be responsible for each type of design. It can be useful to list the groups or individuals who will be consulted in developing the design; draw up an iterative plan for revising the design during the implementation lifecycle. There is a wealth of information about this issue in the 'MLE design' section of *Creating an MLE* (JISC, 2003).

Step 4: identify priorities for development

The plan for implementation for your MLE will be specific to your institution, stakeholders and strategy. A strategy driven by LIS is likely to focus on those areas that are of most relevance to the core business of LIS, such as information management, user support and information skills.

Currier, Brown and Ekmekioglu (2001) present a useful vision for an integrated online learning environment:

- seamless, one-stop access
- all library functions online
- individualization for the learner
- flexibility for the teacher
- universal accessibility
- ease of use.

Involvement by library and information services in MLE development may be within a single area, or may span several. It is important to ensure that all relevant links have been explored. In Scenario 1 (page 8), the most obvious areas for possible integration are:

- library management systems integrated with student information systems
- content management systems integrated with online learning systems
- digital collections, datasets, journals and so on integrated with online learning systems

- web resources such as guides to information literacy and information gateways integrated with online learning systems.

When the systems that might be integrated have been identified, consider which data between the systems should be aligned. For example, at the University of Ulster, a common data schema is used across library, student record and learning environment systems so that information can be integrated between the three. The common data set is based on module number and student number (Uhomoibhi, Masson and Norris, 2003).

It may be useful to review the library services and information sources that are currently available. To what extent are they linked together in a coherent way? Is there potential to link them with other user systems such as those provided by the teaching departments, or the student support services? If so, which of the three scenarios fits best, or do you wish to achieve a combination of all three?

Let us assume that the MLE has been or is to be developed to follow one of the three scenarios described above. We can see a role for library and information systems in all of them. LIS will have a key role to play in the first two scenarios. Scenario 1 focuses specifically on the learning aspects of a MLE. In this case, it is essential that the LIS works closely with the learning providers (usually academic or teaching departments) to integrate a full range of information support into learning activities. This may be done more easily in an e-learning environment than in a traditional environment, but with a new environment it can be more difficult to ensure that all levels of support are provided.

In the recent SCONUL publication *Information Support for E-learning: principles and practice* (SCONUL, 2004), emphasis is placed on the need to include information support in all e-learning provision. The publication sets out useful guidelines that provide a good starting point for colleagues in other departments when MLEs are being designed and the role of information staff considered. The main areas to consider are 'responsibility; quality; equity; access to information and help; information literacy; integration; communication and whole-process costing'. LIS professionals should be included at all stages of the design, delivery and assessment of e-learning so that they can contribute their expertise to the learner's experience. These headings are useful when considering the range of input that LIS staff can make to the MLE.

The LIS role in Scenario 3 should also be investigated as LIS may potentially make use of a single, authoritative source of student data, a single authentication system or an integrated finance system in order to 'feed' LIS systems.

Plan collaboration with teaching departments

LIS and teaching departments will usually already have developed some processes for working together to manage all types of learning resources, including journals and short-loan collections. In many cases the main focus for working together is through the creation of a reading list by the member of teaching staff for each module. Research has shown, however, that there is not always a shared understanding of the processes involved in the creation of reading lists, when they need to be ready during the academic year, how often they are updated, and so on (LINKer, 2003). In the e-learning environment there is the potential need for considerably increased levels of collaboration between LIS and teaching departments because of the greater number of resources that will be used. You may need to assess your current processes and discuss with your academic colleagues how you can work closely together to plan the provision of e-learning resources. This may have many positive benefits. Research at the University of Ulster has shown increased levels of use for e-learning resources when they are integrated into learning environments (Uhomoibhi, Masson and Norris, 2003).

The following sub-sections describe some of the main areas where LIS may need to plan collaboration with colleagues in teaching departments and support units.

Copyright and intellectual property rights

LIS will typically have a long history and much experience of the management of the licensing of resources that are supplied by publishers and others. In the new e-learning environment, many teaching departments and individual academics are not aware of the constraints of copyright and intellectual property rights (IPR); there is sometimes a common belief that any digital objects can be shared freely within the education community. As part of the collaboration between LIS and teaching departments in the provision of e-learning resources, LIS should provide teaching departments with guidance on copyright and IPR legislation, and advise them on appropriate use of resources. The guidance needs to encompass national legislation and local policy, processes and procedures; for example, whether there are budget restraints on the acquisition of digital resources, and whether there are LIS staff with responsibility for copyright clearance (LINKer, 2003).

E-learning resource management

For content creation, access and management to be successful within the MLE, stakeholders in LIS and teaching departments in all three areas must discuss and agree which functions and technologies are needed. LIS will be able to bring its expertise in large-scale collection management, assessment and collection policies, preservation, metadata and good business practices into the e-learning sphere to ensure that appropriate information management practice is followed.

Current e-learning systems have variable provision for the creation and management of e-learning resources. The main difficulty with many e-learning systems from an LIS perspective is that content within the systems is often created and managed according to the module or course structure (such as Psychology module 101, week 5) rather than by subject categories. This severely restricts the potential to cross-reference e-learning resources that are stored within the e-learning system, so resources may be duplicated in several systems.

Not only does this waste storage space but it also greatly increases the burden of resource management and the potential for breaches of copyright and IPR.

Reviews of the use of VLEs have shown that there is often poor resource description within e-learning systems and a lack of shared understanding of the role of LIS in helping to describe resources (LINKer, 2003). If e-learning is to be scaleable and sustainable over a period of time, issues such as resource description need to be considered. LIS has a particularly important role to play in directing or informing this process.

Resource description of e-learning resources

There is a large range of e-learning resources that may be included in a learning environment. These may be developed by the academic, bought, or 'acquired' from the internet or elsewhere (for example, from CD-ROMs).

For LIS professionals, the value and purpose of metadata in describing e-learning materials hardly needs to be emphasized. There is particular motivation for using metadata in e-learning systems. First, such use can encourage the sharing and re-use of objects that have been created in other learning and teaching situations (re-use of materials is not a common model for traditional teaching situations); secondly, it can feed into 'intelligent' systems that may use metadata associated with learning materials to locate resources that match a particular learner's preferences or ambitions.

Current e-learning systems have variable provision for the creation and management of metadata. In some systems, metadata about e-learning resources can be created from a restricted vocabulary and stored separately from the objects. In most cases, metadata can be defined using their own choice of terms by users and is stored with the learning resources in the system (thus is difficult or impossible to search from outside a particular course). Most worryingly, in many cases teachers are not creating metadata for their learning materials either because they are not aware of the value of this, or because the functionality is not available to them (McLean, 2000). LIS has a valuable role in the provision of its expertise in collection description and should advise teaching departments on the importance of metadata creation and management.

Learning objects

There is a lot of debate around the definition of what constitutes a learning object and no clear consensus has been reached. The biggest controversy is about the scope of a learning object – is it a single resource such as a video clip or an overview of a seminar, is it a whole class, or even a whole module? These differences of opinion are not going to be resolved easily, but from a pragmatic perspective we can agree that many of the same issues will apply whether a learning object is a discrete resource of a single media type, or if it is a composite of multiple resources. The main concern from a LIS perspective is that of metadata. For our purposes, all learning materials are described under the broad heading of learning objects – that is, digital resources of any type that are intended to be used in a learning or teaching situation.

Existing metadata standards such as Dublin Core are not felt to be sufficiently detailed to describe learning objects, so new standards for the description of learning objects are emerging, in particular the international Learning Object Metadata standard (LOM). LOM was used as the basis for the most widely known learning object description system, the Sharable Content Object Reference Model (SCORM), which was developed for the US Department of Defence. SCORM is being used for large-scale training systems such as the University of Industry, but is used less widely in higher education.

The Centre for Educational Technology Interoperability Standards has worked in the UK to define a UK-specific subset of terms called the UK Learning Object Metadata (UK LOM Core). LIS staff are advised to examine this specification when they make decisions about learning object metadata (CETIS, 2004).

Provision of access to e-learning resources

LIS will be involved in presenting resources to the user through e-learning systems such as VLEs or through portals and also in providing content to users, either through dedicated user interfaces or from hyperlinks within e-learning systems. It is useful here to refer again to the MLE architecture diagram developed by Becta (see Figure 1.1, page 6). In this diagram, content creation, management and access cross all three levels. Common services such as authentication and authorization and directory services are used to get resources from the content system to the end-user interface. Many of these functions will be shared with research systems as well (McLean and Lynch, 2004).

Access through e-learning systems (as in Scenario 1, page 8)

Learners may often access learning resources through the e-learning system. In a typical scenario, the learner will access a set of course resources that a teacher has prepared to supplement a particular module. Within the resources, the teacher will direct the learner to some supporting e-learning resources. These may be stored locally, within the e-learning software, within the content management system or digital repository, or within other local databases for licensed software; or stored remotely either from a content provider (such as a publisher) or from a website.

E-learning systems offer a variety of methods for accessing remote systems. Some are closely integrated with library management software, and seamless links from the online course to a resource within the library system can be easily created and accessed. For others, the user will be led by hyperlink to a separate search interface from where they can attempt to locate the resource. There are varying views on whether the learner should always have 'one stop' access to all resources. Some information professionals and academics are concerned that providing all information to learners from a single interface reduces their information skills and restricts the choices that they can make about learning resources. Others argue that it should be as simple as possible for busy learners to access the resources that are essential for their learning; they are free to locate additional resources if they wish (Currier, Brown and Ekmekioglu, 2001). Clearly, there are problems with the second approach if the learner needs specialist information to locate the resource, has to re-authenticate several times or only has access to the resource from particular locations, such as within the university network.

It is important to note that technical integration will need to take place on a number of levels. For example, a teacher may wish for the student to access a particular article within an electronic journal rather than simply getting to the main page for the whole journal (McLean and Lynch, 2004).

At the University of Ulster, the Library Service Point (LSP) is a type of 'middleware' that provides integration of the library services into the virtual learning environment. The LSP automatically presents the student with the right information for them based on their profile. These services are based on different information about the student: some are based on their faculty membership, some based on the modules that they are studying, some are based on their student identification number. Information about the student is stored and maintained centrally, so it can be used reliably to give access to services. An example given in Uhomoibhi, Masson and Norris (2003) shows students having access to:

- the main library website and catalogue (generic)
- My Module Resource List (module-specific)
- library information and services for student's faculty (faculty-specific)
- My Electronic Information Services (Athens)(person-specific)
- new additions to the library in student's subject and past exam papers for this module (module-specific)
- My Library Account (person-specific).

In order to achieve this type of integration, the VLE is automatically linking to several other systems: the Athens database, the student record system (that also contains module data) and the library management system. This integration was planned at the design stage for the system.

Where to store resource descriptions

Given that learning environments generally have poor provision for resource descriptions, LIS may wish to take responsibility for this management. There are two main options for the storage and management of resource descriptions: either to use the current library management system or catalogue, or to use a separate digital repository.

Increasingly, LIS includes some digital resources within its main catalogue. Depending on the functionality of the cataloguing system, and the cataloguing policy, there may already be references to some digital resources such as journals in the catalogue. However, it is unlikely that the cataloguing system will contain the right range of functionality for it to be used as the only source of information about learning resources. Usually these will need to be stored and managed as part of the digital repository. However, one of the most thorny issues to tackle when putting in place content management systems is how to link these to other cataloguing systems. Which data should be stored in the digital repository and which should be stored in the catalogue?

In practice, the approach to take depends on your local policy and the functionality of your systems. Do you already have in place federated search facilities? Does the library catalogue allow hyperlinking to external resources? If so, does it use a system of unique identifiers? It is likely that your systems' administrator will have encountered this issue already when considering how to link together your catalogue with internal or external digital collections, so there may be a tried and tested approach that you can follow.

The University of Ulster has taken an innovative approach to the integration of library systems and library services into their VLE. They assume that access to some of the library services and content will come from the VLE. Instead of the user linking directly to a list of digital resources, such as the catalogue, electronic journals and datasets, they are directed to a central service that then re-directs them to online support services or resources (4i project, 2003).

Links to the library management system

In some cases, the library catalogue may be fully integrated with the MLE and cross-searching functions may be simple to put in place. The level of integration that is possible will be dictated by two factors. First, by the technology used for each system – some technologies can be easily integrated and can 'talk to each other', while others cannot. Secondly, by the way that resources are classified and described. For example, if subjects are not recorded within the learning system, it will be not be possible to automatically link to library resources that are linked by subject.

Where the library catalogue is not fully integrated into the MLE it is important to make decisions about how the catalogue will reference from the e-learning system, and at what level the links will appear. Should a link accompany every page within the system or appear at key points, such as within the links to further reading?

Digital repositories

Digital repositories are being hailed by many as a solution to the problem of how to manage, describe and access many different types of resources including e-learning resources. Digital repositories are an essential area for collaboration between LIS and learning and teaching providers. Many popular e-learning systems will 'lock' content into their software, so it cannot be easily reviewed, re-used, or linked to from other systems such as library catalogues. There is a growing desire to store resources outside the e-learning system in a neutral repository, where resources can be properly described and managed (McLean and Lynch, 2004).

The types of functions that we would expect to see in a repository would be content discovery through searching and browsing, content management and content description to allow the addition of standard metadata and other cataloguing information. We might also find content aggregation (where separate learning objects can be aggregated into groups of objects) and the ability to discover resources from other repository systems through cross-searching tools (McLean and Lynch, 2004).

There are increasing numbers of commercial and free repository systems available and their deployment should be considered within the framework of the institution's information strategy. Ideally, an institution would use a single repository to manage all its varied range of digital assets. In practical terms, it should be recognized that different types of resources will typically be used in different ways, and this may affect the type of repository that is needed. It is generally believed that a more realistic vision for the future is that every institution will deploy a number of different repositories, but will use standard interfaces between the systems so that they can link together and be cross-searched (McLean and Lynch, 2004).

Federated searching

Federated searching is closely associated with digital repositories and distributed content. It is an important method to increase the level of integration between library services and learning environments by providing a single search access point to a number of different resources stored either remotely or locally. Most federated search engines or software use the Z39.50 protocol. They may be used to perform searches across a range of resource types, from catalogues to full-text articles.

There is increasing interest in enabling federated searches of digital repositories at learning object level but this is predicated upon learning object metadata being read by search engines. This is not possible from within most search engines, apart from specialized learning object management software, which is not usually capable of providing searches of traditional e-resources. The Open Archive Initiative has produced a protocol for metadata harvesting that makes it possible to interrogate and retrieve metadata from digital repositories.

This makes cross-searching of learning object repositories possible (Open Archives Initiative, 2002), but this protocol has not yet been widely deployed.

If the search engine is able to cross-search different resources at different levels of information (that is, catalogue record, abstract, object metadata, full-text), the system designer needs to consider that collection descriptions may be inconsistent across repositories (Open Archives Forum, 2003) and users will need guidance on how to interpret results of federated searches.

Access through portals (for Scenario 2, page 9)

With a less integrated approach, learners may access learning resources from within an institutional or LIS portal. LIS may already provide its own portal or gateway to learning resources within the institution that will provide a single 'jumping off point' to resources such as the library catalogue, annotated lists of subject resources, Athens authenticated access to subscribed journals, and so on. If there is not the case, LIS may wish to take ownership of the learning resource aspect of the portal, or at least to have input to the design of the interface and the guidance that is provided to users to ensure that it conforms to appropriate standards and is consistent with the LIS documentation.

Access management, authentication and authorization

There may also be potential to develop shared systems between departments. International research shows that there are some common sets of information and common functions that are needed by numerous different systems – and it would make more sense to use a single source of information rather than several separate and parallel ones. One example is authentication and authorization systems – users generally have to re-authenticate with separate user names and passwords for each different system that they use, such as for Athens, for the virtual learning environment, and to access their library account. It makes sense to consider developing a shared authentication system that can be used by all systems. Not only does it make life easier for the users, but it also reduces the amount of administration required to keep up-to-date user records – particularly if the authentication system can be connected to the student record system, and automatically updated daily with accurate information. Studies have shown the providing 'single sign-on' to multiple resources may greatly reduce the number of user queries received by user support and help desk within LIS, which reduces costs and improves efficiency (Uhomoibhi, Masson and Norris, 2003).

Conclusion

The move towards support of learning and teaching through online environments and greater consideration of integrated access to resources from across a range of university or college departments may provide both an opportunity and a threat for library and information services. LIS has expertise in information description, information management and user support that puts it in a strong position to either lead on an integrated e-systems approach or to contribute to activities that are already underway. There is no single MLE model or objectives for the development of a MLE: the development of a MLE is specific to an organization or group of organizations. Strategic planning is needed at the start, with participation from all major stakeholders, to ensure that planning and implementation will meet the most important shared objectives. Such objectives may include the desire to support e-learning, to support end-users better, to improve admin-istrative processes or a combination of factors. In all cases, the role of LIS should be carefully considered in order to maximize invest-ment in library systems and to improve user support.

References

4i project (2003) *Approach to VLE-Library Integration*, Belfast, University of Ulster, www.ulst.ac.uk/library/4i/deliverables/outputs/4i%20Approach. pdf.

Allison, C. (2003) *INSIDE Final Report*, Bristol, Joint Information Systems Committee, www.jiscinfonet.ac.uk/Resources/external-resources/INSIDErep/view.

Bouch, G. and Wilks, S. (2002) *Pilgrim's Progress: the University of Plymouth student portal*, Boulder, Educause.

Centre for Educational Technology Interoperability Standards (2004) *UK Learning Object Metadata Core*, Draft 0.2, Bolton, CETIS, www.cetis.ac.uk/profiles/uklomcore.

Currier, S., Brown, S. and Ekmekioglu, C. (2001) *INSPIRAL, INveStigating Portals for Information Resources And Learning: final report*, Strathclyde, Strathclyde University, inspiral.cdlr.strath.ac.uk/documents/INSPfinrep.doc.

Dolphin, I. and Sherratt, R (2003) *Developing Port.hull – The University of Hull Portal: a JISC case study*, Hull, University of Hull.

Education for Change (2003) *Study of MLE Activity*, Bristol, Joint Information Systems Committee, www.jisc.ac.uk/project_mle_activity.html.

Joint Information Systems Committee (2003) *Creating an MLE*, Bristol, JISC, www.jiscinfonet.ac.uk/InfoKits/InfoKits/creating-an-mle/.

LINKer (2003) *Linking Digital Libraries and Virtual Learning Environments: evaluation and review, final report: formative evaluation of the DiVLE Programme*, Bristol, Joint Information Systems Committee, www.jisc.ac.uk/uploaded_documents/Linker-d5-MASTER.doc.

McLean, N. (2000) *Library Services for a Managed Learning Environment*, Sydney, Mcquarie University, www.lib.mq.edu.au/conference/mclean/managed/.

McLean, N. and Lynch, C. (2004) *Interoperability between Information and Learning Environments – Bridging the Gaps* (in draft), Burlington, IMS Global Consortium, www.imsglobal.org/DLims_white_paper_publicdraft_1.pdf.

Office of National Statistics (2004) *Living in Britain – General Household Survey 2002*, Norwich, HMSO.

Open Archives Forum (2003) *OAI for Beginners, the Open Archives Forum Online Tutorial*, Open Archives Forum, www.oaforum.org/.

Open Archives Initiative (2002) *The Open Archives Initiative Protocol for Metadata Harvesting*, Open Archives Initiative, www.openarchives.org/OAI/2.0/openarchivesprotocol.htm.

Society of College, National and University Libraries (2004) *Information Support for E-learning: principles and practice*, London, SCONUL, www.sconul.ac.uk/pubs_stats/pubs/pubs/info_support_ elearning.pdf.

Uhomoibhi, C., Masson, A. and Norris, L. (2003) Integrating VLE and library systems: opportunities and challenges, *Informatica*, **23** (3).

2

Process and partnerships

Oleg Liber

Introduction

Higher education (HE) has undergone massive changes in the last few decades, changes which have had a huge impact on the organization and operation of higher education institutions (HEIs). Student numbers entering higher education have risen to 40%, while per capita funding has dropped significantly in real terms. Inevitably this has had a major impact on teaching and learning within higher education; not only has the student body become more diverse, with a wider range of needs, but class sizes have become larger, making it more difficult for teachers to respond to these needs. At the same time the pressure has been increased on institutions to attract ever larger numbers of students to remain viable, and then to retain these students. Heavy financial penalties are imposed by funding councils to force institutions to address the problem of student retention.

In parallel to these structural changes, the explosion of internet technologies has raised the possibility of transforming the way in which many practices within higher education take place, but poses the problem of how they can be incorporated into long established structures and processes at a time of great institutional stress. Nevertheless, institutions are looking for potential solutions to their problems based on these new technologies, new pedagogic practices, and new organizational processes and structures, each influencing the other. Technology is variously seen as (a) improving access (and taking pressure off the physical estate) by allowing study to take place off campus, at a time and place that suits the particular student; (b) improving quality, enabling students to have access to better materials and educational interactions, and responding to the wider demands of the diverse student body; or (c) reducing costs, by automating some of the previously human intensive processes.

It would be fair to say that there is little evidence of whether technology has delivered on any of these aspirations in education. Nevertheless, new e-learning systems and materials continue to be developed, and technology-supported learning is being adopted at a rate unimaginable a decade earlier. But as systems are implemented within institutions, existing processes are disrupted in unanticipated ways, leading to further technical and managerial interventions as institutions struggle to exploit technology better in order to realize their aims.

The combination of the changing social, financial, educational and technical contexts encourages practitioners to question every aspect of how higher education institutions carry out their business, and calls into question the inter-related responsibilities of academic, service and administrative departments, and management. This chapter explores how managers in institutions can begin to understand these responsibilities and thereby develop a structured approach to organizational change.

The organization of higher education institutions

Universities and other higher education institutions have evolved structures and processes over many years that are suited to a previous, more elitist model of higher education, when students were selected according to their A-level results, were predominantly in their late teens, full time and planned to live on campus. Courses ran within well defined academic years, curricula tended to offer few choices, and teaching methods were pretty uniform – lectures, some tutorials and in some subjects labs and field work, with the relatively static supporting technologies of lecture theatres, laboratories, books, libraries and so on. The situation today is very different. Students are seen much more as customers – they now contribute to their fees; their age profile is much more varied; there are far more part-time students, and many live at home. Widening access has led to universities being increasingly concerned with recruitment and retention of students. Curriculum design and teaching methods are having to be adapted to respond to the changing circumstances.

The changes outlined above have put great pressure on institutions to adapt their processes, and the responsibility to develop and implement these changes is usually given to service departments. An important example of this is the increased pressure on academic computing services to make student registration, authentication, information recording and certification work more efficiently in response to widening participation; another example is the ever growing demand on computing services to provide new facilities as students demand access from home using their own computers; a third is the expectation that libraries adapt their services to provide and support increasingly digitized resources. These can be seen as piecemeal responses to a changing educational context, seeking to use technology to paper over cracks in the institutional fabric. However, there are limits to how long this strategy can work; at some point a strategic approach to organizational change will be needed, which will involve the use of technologies in an integrated and cross institutional way.

The development of learning technologies

The development of learning technologies over the last 20 years has had a considerable impact on higher education and on how institutions organize themselves. It can be roughly divided into three overlapping phases: the multimedia phase, the internet phase and the virtual learning environment (VLE) phase, which includes the development of managed learning environments (MLEs).

The multimedia phase

The multimedia phase was primarily concerned with producing computer-based materials in the belief that at least part of the curriculum could be delivered through these materials. Being based on the personal computer, the focus was very much on single learners, and considerable effort was put into developing theories and methods for the design and development of individualized materials. During this period, terms like multimedia, hypertext, hypermedia and interactivity became popular, and it was felt that computer-based materials offered potentially significant benefits over linear-paper-based materials, since they could allow a degree of adaptation to learner actions.

However, this phase was characterized by limited technical resources in universities – there were not enough computers of a high enough specification to run these materials. There was also insufficient experience within institutions to understand the role these materials could play and to support academic staff in their use. It was difficult to identify exactly how learners should have access to these materials – during timetabled sessions? In their private study time? Who should support them? Academic staff or library staff?

Despite these problems, this period was important in that many institutions first identified the need for and employed dedicated learning technologists, albeit usually on short term contracts and with external funding from programmes like the Teaching and Learning Technology Programme (TLTP). Many of these people have now been working in universities for some considerable time, often having moved to more senior university positions. Distribution of learning materials produced by funded projects was also a problem. Materials were typically produced on CD-ROMs, and so copies had to be made, marketed and sufficient copies sold to make the enterprise worthwhile. Very few of the projects that were funded to develop materials succeeded in tackling these problems, and the market was too small for commercial success.

The internet phase

The internet phase of learning technologies probably began when the first graphical web browser (the National Center for Supercomputing Application's Mosaic) became available. Universities had been using the internet for some years, but mainly for e-mail and specific scientific endeavours. The graphical web suddenly made the internet interesting and accessible to a wider group, and there was a tremendous explosion of new websites established by enthusiastic academics, containing learning resources, working papers and other materials – all freely available, often running on Macintosh-based servers.

Interest in the use of the internet and the web grew enormously, and as it grew, so technologies improved. For example, e-mail clients became easier to use, and allowed for access to newsgroups, which began to be used increasingly as discussion forums for modules and courses in universities. Other tools began to emerge, like chat rooms, or internet-based video conferencing (CU-SeeMe). All of these provided the components for the next phase of learning technology development, virtual learning environments or learning management systems (LMS). (Interestingly, the emergence of the internet resulted in a backward step for learning content, since it was impossible or impractical to display or run advanced content, for example online simulations. Much early learning content that was available on the web tended to be text with some images and, of course, hyperlinks. Only recently with the later releases of tools like Macromedia's Flash have interactive learning materials returned to the level of sophistication they were at in the early 1990s.)

The virtual learning environment phase

For those who were proficient at making web pages and designing websites, the web and the other internet-based tools were enough for them to set up interesting online learning environments for their courses. They could structure and present materials, hand-craft assessments, incorporate discussion and e-mail groups, and use various other tools to create their own unique online systems (Holyfield et al., 1995). However, this was only ever going to be a minority sport; for most people, without technical skills or great enthusiasm, to engage in using the internet within their teaching, simpler tools were needed that offered a range of facilities in an easy-to-use way.

In the mid-1990s systems were developed that brought together the separate facilities that were becoming popular on the web – incorporating web content, discussion forums, student lists, grade-books, multiple choice testing and various other features into a single system, often employing a classroom metaphor. Encouraged by the dot.com bubble and with a strong push from the Joint Information Systems Committee (JISC) and the funding councils, these systems, known as LMS in the USA and VLEs in the UK were rapidly adopted by many institutions, whose senior management saw them as a quick solution to the adoption and exploitation of e-learning, which they had been told could solve their problems of widening access and pedagogic diversity.

There is no doubt that VLEs have had a major impact on the main-streaming of learning technologies – almost every HEI and further education (FE) college has one (or more). However, while extend-ing access, they have created their own problems. First, lecturers did not want to have to type in the names of all their students into their VLE, which resulted in much technical work in getting student information from student record systems to VLEs (and increased demand on computing services). Secondly, their use had a major impact on existing administrative processes within institutions. For example, registration procedures had to be tightened up to ensure that when VLEs were populated with student lists, they were accurate – there have been many experiences when this has not been the case. In a classroom-based course, a student can still attend even if there has been an error or delay in their registration. With a VLE, they would be denied all access. This and other adoption issues with the use of VLEs have had a disruptive effect – there have been benefits and costs.

Managed learning environments

As a response to the problem of integrating VLEs with other institutional systems like student record systems, JISC established its MLE programmes (JISC, 2004c). These funded a range of projects and experiments that explored technical and organizational aspects of incorporating VLEs into institutions, and JISC continues to support initiatives concerning MLEs. Its JISC InfoNet service has a specific remit to support the sector with MLE adoption, and as part of the service it hosts a large set of materials on its website known as the 'Creating an MLE' Infokit (Liber and Holyfield, 2003). These materials were developed by a group of leading experts in e-learning and learning technology, and incorporate resources developed by all MLE-programme-funded projects. At the time of writing, many institutions are grappling with the technical and organizational aspects of MLE implementation, with varying degrees of success (see Chapter 1).

A key issue in MLE implementation is interoperability – getting different technical systems to be able to understand, exchange and appropriately use each other's data. This applies in a range of ways. Content interoperability is concerned with being able to use learning materials developed for one VLE within another. Learner information interoperability is concerned with learner information contained on one student record system being accessible and interpretable by other record systems and by VLEs, library systems and so on. Interoperability can be achieved on a bespoke basis – so for example, a specific VLE can be made to interoperate with a specific student record system within a particular institution. This typically involves lots of work for suppliers (which they are pleased to charge high rates for!) but makes institutions very dependent on them, and the cost of changing component systems locks them in to existing systems, making adaptation difficult. The alternative approach is to insist that all suppliers adopt internationally agreed interoperability standards. Learning content that is packaged in a standard way can be shipped between VLEs and repositories that conform to the standard. Student information that has a standard format and means of exchange can be easily transferred between systems that have implemented the standard. Clearly, adopting standards, while representing an initial overhead for system developers, provides far more flexibility for institutions.

Interoperability standards

JISC has long recognized the need for interoperability standards. All of its MLE programmes require that funded projects implement interoperability standards where they exist, and it has established a Centre for Educational Technology Interoperability Standards (CETIS) as a service to the HE and FE sectors. CETIS represents JISC on national and international efforts to establish e-learning standards, advises JISC and higher and further education, and engages the community in this work through its special interest groups (SIGs), where institutions can participate in defining their requirements and testing specifications for new standards.

There are currently specifications for standards in the following areas:

- *metadata*: how learning content should be described for easy searching
- *content packaging*: how content should be packaged to allow it to be moved between systems
- *question and test interoperability*: how assessment should be defined to allow users to move between computer-based assessment systems
- *learner information packaging*: a standard set of fields for learner information to allow interoperability
- *enterprise*: a standardized way for transferring enrolments and later returning results to facilitate student record system and VLE interoperability.

Work continues in all of these areas and also into standards and profiles for accessibility, portfolios and other aspects of e-learning.

Detailed information on these can be found on the CETIS website (www.cetis.ac.uk).

JISC has promoted and supported the use of interoperability standards as they emerge, making the UK the leading country in the adoption of standards. As well as funding the CETIS service, JISC is funding the development of tools and systems that facilitate the adoption of standards. Its recent Exchange for Learning (X4L) programme (JISC, 2004a) has funded the development of a range of standards-based learning resources as well as three systems that help with the use of interoperability standards: RELOAD, an application for tagging content with metadata and then creating interoperable content packages; JORUM, building repositories for interoperable content; and TOIA, a standards-based assessment system.

As has been suggested, interoperability standards reduce the costs of integration, facilitate continuous MLE development and thus help institutions avoid becoming locked in to particular systems, since learning materials and student information can be transferred to other systems. However, the total cost of ownership of systems – the purchase or licensing costs, training and support costs – makes it difficult for institutions to provide central support to more than a single VLE. This raises a number of problems. First, it limits pedagogic flexibility; it has been argued that VLEs embody a specific approach to learning and teaching, which may not suit all subjects, teachers or learners. Secondly, it reduces differentiation between institutions – a chemistry course using System X at one institution can look very similar to a chemistry course using System X in any other institution – especially if they also reuse available learning materials. There are signs that as teachers become accustomed to using VLEs, they are beginning to become critical of the limitations they impose. Thirdly, VLEs replicate a number of functions that other institutional systems already have – for example user authentication.

The E-learning Framework Programme

As a response to these issues, JISC has launched its E-learning Framework Programme (JISC, 2004b). This is based on a service-oriented architecture (SOA) approach with a focus on web-service technology, where specific functionality can be provided by an application over the web to another application. So, for example, messaging services like discussion forums can be made available for use within other applications, like a VLE, removing the need for large monolithic, jack-of-all-trades applications. The idea behind the framework programme is that if all functions needed within an institution's MLE could be defined as web services, it would remove the duplication of functions like authentication, and would allow learning applications like VLEs to be assembled from several web services, depending on the needs of the particular course or pedagogic approach. This represents a radical step in the development of learning technology, made possible by the establishment of XML as a standard, and the emergence of a Web Service Description Language (WSDL) standard. It also serves to protect investment in existing systems by exposing their internal functionality through a service interface. This allows other applications to build on and use, rather than replicate, this technology.

These developments will once again have a major impact on how institutions carry out their business, offering efficiency and pedagogic benefits, but requiring adaptation on the part of information and computing services. JISC is funding the development of the framework and of software tools that can make specific web services a reality. It is also funding research into the pedagogy of e-learning to inform the technical development.

Inevitably the adoption of the E-learning Framework will have serious implications for universities. On the one hand, it should eliminate duplication of effort, and allow for more choice. Departments will be able to define different learning environments using various web services suited to their subject and teaching approaches. On the other hand, information services departments will have to manage a set of new technologies, and help academic departments to exploit the benefits they offer. This will require new skills on the part of staff, including user interface design. The introduction of new technologies always brings with them the need for accompanying changes in the organization and in staff roles and responsibilities.

Of course it may be that institutions decide not to adopt the new e-learning framework approach, although the evidence from the USA is that universities are beginning to develop similar approaches, specifically within the SAKAI project (SAKAI, 2004), where several leading universities are jointly developing a SOA, component-based MLE. But whatever happens with this programme, we can be sure that technology will continue to evolve and offer new opportunities for teaching, learning, support and administration. The challenge for universities is to be able to adapt their processes continuously to benefit from the opportunities without destabilizing their existing procedures. Inevitably it will be information and library service departments that will be expected to play a leading part in helping institutional change, and at the same time transform the services they offer to respond to these changes. The next section suggests a method by which a whole institution can address the challenge of organizational and technological change, which involves stakeholders from every part of the organization.

The process of change

The impact of new external pressures on higher education discussed earlier, of increased student numbers and reduced per capita funding, and of rapidly changing learning technologies that directly affect their primary activities, demand that HEIs respond creatively to these challenges. These changes put pressure on every aspect of their operation, and no department, academic or service, will be unaffected. The typical response to gradual change is to make small adaptations to existing practice – increase class sizes, buy extra copies of key text books, hire extra administrative staff, and so on. But at a certain point this approach fails, and radical changes have to be made, both in academic and administrative structures and processes.

The demands on the estate, for example, may require major changes in teaching approaches, involving larger but fewer lectures, and more private study; or pressures on computing resources may result in the redesign of library spaces. The danger is that these changes may be implemented in an ad hoc fashion, where changes in one area can result in increased stress in another. It is important that when significant change to an institution's organization and processes is needed that it is founded on a well elaborated model of change. The following questions need to be addressed:

- Why is change needed?
- What are current institutional processes and what are their problems?
- What organizational and technological changes might resolve these problems?
- What technologies are currently available that might help?

These questions need to be richly elaborated, and should ideally be considered by contributors from all stakeholders in the institutions. Unsurprisingly they closely parallel the first four sections of the JISC resource 'Creating an MLE' (Liber and Holyfield, 2003), since many institutions are looking to new technologies to help them manage the challenges described above. Only when these questions have been fully explored can the process of implementing change take place. The answers to these questions cannot be provided here, but suggestions as to how they might be addressed follow below.

Why is change needed?

The external pressures on higher education, although common to all institutions, will be experienced differently depending on an individual institution's identities. There is significant diversity between universities in the UK higher education sector, with varying emphases on teaching and learning, research and enterprise activities. Some have a regional focus, others see themselves as nationally focused and others are international players. Some embrace specific models of teaching and learning, others provide for diverse approaches. These and other factors make it important for universities to elaborate their identities with some care.

The following categories come from Espejo, Bowling and Hoverstadt's cybernetic methodology for studying organizations and contribute to an overall identity statement (1999, 661–78). They have some similarity to Checkland's soft systems methodology (1999), but where his CATWOE is concerned with the identification of problems, Espejo et al's TASCOI is concerned with organizational identity:

- *Transformation.* What are the key transformations that the institution is trying to achieve – to create new graduates? To create new knowledge through research? To support regional development through knowledge transfer? What is the balance between these?
- *Actors.* Who are the key people in achieving these transformations? This may seem a trivial question, but in fact the answers reveal the institution's view of the learning process. For example, are students actors in creating their learning? Or are they customers (see below)? Or both? Discussing this question reveals pedagogic orientations which in turn impact on how learning is organized.
- *Suppliers.* Who supplies the material that enables the transformation? In HEIs this can refer to knowledge – but is this contained in texts from publishers, or learning objects from other institutions, or raw data gathered by researchers? It could also refers to students – where do they come from (local, national, overseas)? Is this changing? Again, answers to this question help to elaborate the differences between institutions.
- *Customers.* Who are the beneficiaries of the transformation? Students? Government? Society? The local economy?
- *Owners.* Who ultimately controls the transformation? The governors? Senate? Council? The funding council?

- *Intervenors.* Who are the significant others that impact on the operation of the institution? Other HEIs? Regional development agencies? Research councils? Others?

These questions are intended to stimulate a structured discussion and elaboration of the purpose and identity of the institution in its current situation. In the process of examining these, questions of how effectively each is being realized will emerge. For example, is the balance between teaching, research and enterprise changing, and is this being managed properly? Is the student body changing? Are knowledge sources changing? Are competitors and collaborators changing? Is the overall identity fixed or can it change? What impact will adopting e-learning have? How should it be adopted?

Organizations the size of universities are structured and have academic departments, almost always based on subjects, and service or administrative departments, such as finance, personnel, estates or library and computing services. In some cases another layer may be inserted, that of the faculty, bringing together a number of subjects. For example, a faculty of science might contain separate physics, chemistry and biology departments, each with its own head of department, and with a dean as head of the faculty. Service departments provide common services to every department, but in some cases customized to an individual department's needs. Registry provides services to do with student recruitment, student records and certification, which is pretty standard for all departments. The library might provide separate library services for each department, or may offer a single centralized library, depending on the size and organization of the institution.

Each of these departments, academic or service and administrative, have their own purposes and identities, and it is worth exploring and elaborating these using the TASCOI model (see Table 2.1, page 44). For academic departments there will be a degree of variation from the institution's responses to each category, and these are worth exploring in some detail. Departments may have very different student bodies, for example, with some having far more overseas students than others. However, every academic department's responses to the TASCOI questions will be subsumed within the institution's responses. The transformation will be the same, but will be directly relevant to the specific subject under consideration. The actors within the department should be a subset of the actors within the institution. However, if there is a major difference, for example if the institution includes students as actors, and a department doesn't, this reveals a difference in educational philosophy which may need further exploration between senior and departmental management and staff.

Variations between departments and the overall institution's statement can reveal underlying issues, which in turn can affect the way in which departments may respond to pressures to change. A department whose philosophy is primarily concerned with knowledge transmission may focus its attention on developing and providing better online content to take pressure off its lecturing staff. A department that is more concerned with developing intellectual skills may seek to use technology to support problem- or project-based learning. The TASCOI exercise can reveal these differences, and provide information for the institution on the types of actions it may need to take to respond to pressures for change.

Service department identities

Service departments are likely to produce very different responses to the TASCOI exercise from academic departments. This is because they are not primary centres in the institution, carrying out the institution's mission, but rather regulatory in nature, existing to ensure that there is co-ordination and cohesion in the way primary centres do their business. Table 2.1 shows a comparison of an academic department's and a service (in this case finance) department's possible responses.

Table 2.1   Two responses to a TASCOI exercise

	Academic department	Finance department
T	To transform students into certified graduate level members of their subject community	To enable departments to manage their financial transactions efficiently, effectively and legally
A	Teachers and students within the department	Finance officers and assistants
S	Publishers, libraries and learning object repositories, professional associations	Funding Councils (rules and regulations), financial authorities and associations
C	Students, local economy, industry, national government	Academic departments
O	Governing body, privy council	Governing body, senior management
I	Other academic departments in the university, competing departments elsewhere, local industry, professional associations	Other service departments

Be aware that this is a very abbreviated set of responses – the results of a full blown elaboration would be much more detailed. The point, however, is to demonstrate how different the responses are between the two departments. At one level this is not surprising – one would not expect a finance department to have academic aims. However, it can also be the source of tensions within an organization. Service departments are just that – at the service of the academic aims of the institution. Although poor financial services can damage the success of a university, excellent financial services cannot make a university excellent; only excellence in its primary, its academic, activities can achieve this. Service departments can play a crucial support role in helping academic departments achieve their best – but it is the academic departments themselves that have to do the achieving. However, it is also possible for service departments to be efficient and well organized in the way they pursue their work but to cause problems for academic departments instead of helping them. Insisting on particular bureaucratic methods that suit the service department, but do not fit in well with academic timetables or pressures, for example, can lead to great tensions. On the other hand, staff in academic departments need to understand that service departments are also have limited resources, and so the way the service is provided needs to be negotiated. What is important is that the primary purposes take precedent over regulatory purposes, to the extent that they should be included within regulatory transformation statements – for example, 'To enable departments to manage their financial transactions efficiently, in pursuance of their key aims and objectives'.

The TASCOI exercise can reveal potential problems between service and administrative departments and the academic departments they serve, and help management to devise approaches to resolving these issues.

What are current institutional processes and what are their problems?

The TASCOI exercise can help enormously with elaborating the identity of the institution, which in turn can help with identifying the approach to change that is appropriate for the institution in question. How will widening access impact on the organizational identity? How should technology be used in support of its identity? What sorts of organizational changes are needed so as not undermine the identity? Or does the identity need to change? In what way? These questions and others can emerge from the TASCOI exercise, and establish the agenda for change that is relevant and appropriate for the institution in question. However, this agenda will at this stage be at a high level of generality, and before any process of change can be engaged in, there needs to be a good understanding of the institution in action and its business processes and practices.

There are a number of techniques and methodologies for modelling business processes, some of which require considerable investment of time on the part of those seeking to understand the organization. These can be very useful, but because of their technical nature, they tend to exclude many stakeholders from participating in the exercise. It is not appropriate to elaborate these here, and references to them are provided at the end of this chapter. However, it is crucial to recognize two things: all processes are undertaken by people; and there are many hidden or informal processes that people engage in that solve issues not resolved by formal processes. To understand these properly, people playing key roles in the institution – teaching staff, managers, service staff, administrators – must be given the opportunity to describe their missions, aims, objectives and key tasks. They also need to describe what they require from others to be able to do their job effectively, and the problems they experience in doing their jobs.

Mumford's ETHICS method (1995) offers a structured approach to gathering information from people on their personal views of their roles, responsibilities and requirements. As its title suggests, ETHICS is concerned with the design and adoption of information systems by organizations, but also provides a useful approach to the design of organizational and process changes. Part of ETHICS involves getting the main actors to fill in a questionnaire that contains the following questions:

1   Work mission: what are you striving to achieve in your job?
2   What are your principal key tasks?
3   Which is your most important key task?

For each key task answer the following:

4   What are the principal objectives that the task must achieve?
5   What are the day-to-day or regular activities involved in doing this work?
6   What information do you need for your day-to-day tasks?
7   What are the most serious problems that must be avoided or corrected?
8   What information do you need to solve these problems?
9   What are the critical success factors that determine your ability to carry out this task at a high level of quality?

10   What information do you need to carry out this task at a high level of quality?

11   What new methods, services or tools could help?

12   How do you manage the different elements involved in this task? e.g. what targets do you and others set for this task?

13   What information is needed to check that these targets are being met?

These questions can be answered individually, or better still can form the agenda for a group discussion. They can reveal the actual practice involved in carrying out a range of jobs within the institution, rather than just relying on job definitions, which often do not sufficiently reflect the reality of day-to-day practice. By having the right mix of actors in any group, process problems can be brought to the surface. For example, by having a representative of everyone involved in student registration – academic staff, registry, students, computing services, finance – the problems can be identified and solutions proposed more successfully than through any systems analysis undertaken by a consultant.

Care needs to be taken to ensure that all aspects of a job are covered, including those relating to activities that only take place infrequently. For example, teaching staff may be involved in registration activities at the start of a year or semester, or they might be involved in curriculum development activities at various times. All key tasks need to be included in the responses to the questions. To undertake this for a whole institution is not trivial, and will take some time; but the benefits in process improvement can be significant.

The information gathered can provide a detailed picture of the work of the institution, and identify the problems that people face in doing their jobs. It is important that this information should play an important part in helping shape the nature and process of any proposed changes to the institution's operations.

What organizational and technological changes might resolve these problems?

The previous sections have proposed how an institution can explore its identity and how this is distributed throughout its departments; and how important information on people's roles, tasks and information needs can be gathered. This in turn can be used to develop a rich picture of the important processes that the institution depends on, how they take place, who is involved, and the perceived problems with them. These processes provide the foundation on which decisions on organizational and process changes can be based. It is important that all people involved in them – academic staff, support staff, administrators and students – are able to participate in discussing how existing processes affect or have affected them, and to make proposals about improvements. They also need to be able to consider how and where technology can help with their problems, and where it would not be appropriate.

To this end it is worth revisiting the questions suggested in the previous section, and also to ask after each one:

- How and which technologies can help improve this?
- What organizational changes can improve this?

Asking all stakeholders these questions can often result in a surprising range of positive proposals for change. Replies will have to be aggregated and sifted until a detailed set of changes can be proposed for consideration, and another iteration embarked upon.

The importance of wide involvement in establishing broad requirements for process and organizational change cannot be stressed enough, so that there can be ownership of the change process across the institution. Mumford (1995) suggests that before any new technical system is implemented, a steering group and a design group should be established, with representatives of all stakeholders. The design group has responsibility for arriving at and specifying the technical and organizational changes as described above, and later managing the implementation of the agreed changes, based on the information on objectives, key tasks, information needs and so on gathered earlier. The design of any new organizational processes and technical implementation must reflect these. The eventual objectives produced by the design group must be checked by the wider community and if necessary amended until there is widespread agreement.

The steering group's role is to balance the needs of the different groups, and to make sure that proposed changes are explained and reassurances given about then. Only if this is done properly can there be any hope for trouble-free implementation of organizational and technical changes.

Once broad requirements for changes have been established and agreed, a detailed elaboration of the requirements should take place at all levels and in all departments. There is a range of formal methodologies for requirements gathering, some of which are referenced at the end of this chapter. It is important to stress that the widest possible involvement of stakeholders is advisable in this process, so that all aspects of any proposed changes are fully identified.

What technologies are currently available that might help?

Throughout this chapter it has been stressed that technology should be seen as subservient to the needs of the institution and its members. Properly used it can be of significant benefit; badly implemented it can be disruptive and cause major problems. That is why the major emphasis must be on understanding which problems are to be tackled with technology, and to make sure that technical implementation is accompanied by organizational changes agreed by all stakeholders.

It is important that as discussions about requirements proceed, they are informed by the technical options available to the institution. In the modern world there are increasingly more choices than hitherto. Should only commercial products be used? What about open source software? To what extent will software need to be written for the particular implementation, and what capacity does the institution have to do this? How can the risks of new technology adoption be balanced against the benefits?

It is important that a thorough review of options is made and questions like these are fully addressed. Fortunately external help is available through JISC and others, who provide information and services on precisely these sorts of questions. But in the final analysis technical decisions that are made must be centred on the detailed needs of the institution.

The role of library and information services

Administrative computing, computer services and library services departments have always played multiple roles within universities, and in recent years the work of these three departments has become somewhat entwined. Computer services might provide access to learning materials, previously the role of the library. Library services help students to use computers, and handle online authentication. Administrative computing services provide and manage systems and information on students used by libraries and computing services. Inevitably this has led in many cases to all these services being provided by an amalgamated, single department, with varying degrees of success depending on how well reorganizations have been handled. These departments have also become the home for new e-learning and learning technology units, providing support and advice for departments beginning to use e-learning. These combinations have sometimes been problematic because the critical success factors for each unit can be very different. Those with responsibility for student records are concerned with data accuracy and integrity, and will evaluate any proposed changes against this criterion. Learning technologists are much more concerned with innovation and pedagogy, and can see the caution of academic computing services as an obstacle to their mission. Librarians are concerned with managing learning materials, and may see the unregulated use of online content as destabilizing. Computer services are concerned that the technical infrastructure is sound and secure, and find the demands of ever changing technology problematic.

Unfortunately, information service departments have often not been given enough support and time to go through the processes suggested earlier in this chapter to resolve these internal issues. To make matters worse, they are often expected to advise and take the lead in adopting and implementing new technical systems, often with few extra resources and little staff development. This is clearly problematic, and will severely affect the possibilities of successful implementation. It is of crucial importance that information service departments are given the opportunity, resources and encouragement to make sure that their own internal processes and structure are such that they allow a proper balance between the criteria of people with different responsibilities, so that innovation does not threaten stability or vice-versa. Only then can proper advice be given to academic and other departments on innovations and change.

Information services departments need to recognize that different subject departments may need different e-learning solutions, and find ways to support this. They should help departments to innovate without making costly mistakes, and provide systems that allow safe experimentation, and encourage academic staff to develop their skills and take more responsibility for their own use of technology. When they understand the information needs of lecturers they will be able to negotiate with them how these can best be achieved. This requires the building of trust and understanding between information service departments and academic departments. It is the responsibility of senior management to ensure that this is indeed the case, and the process of engaging in discussing organizational changes suggested earlier in this chapter can have a major impact on helping this to take place, as the critical success factors of different stakeholders are made evident.

Conclusion

Universities are hugely inert bodies. They have been carrying out their missions for many years, and have so far been able to adapt to environmental changes in knowledge, society, economics and so on with minimal change to their organizational processes and structures. If an academic from the 19th century was brought by time machine to the present day, they would still recognize a university, even though some aspects of it would be very different from what they were used to. But the challenges facing universities today brought about by communications technology and globalization are unlike anything universities have had to face hitherto. The explosion of knowledge and information, the number of publications, access to information, the removal of international barriers and economic deregulation are demanding that universities adapt at a rate and in ways as yet unimagined. The challenge is the result of changes in the global information infrastructure made possible by computing and information processing capability; and the response to this challenge will have to make best use of the very same technologies. Inevitably this means that information and computing professionals will have to play a leading role in helping their institutions to adapt and change.

This chapter has argued that change cannot be achieved by technical innovation itself, but must be accompanied by changes in organizational processes and structures. To have the best hope of success, these must involve the widest possible range of participants to identify how and which changes and uses of technology are best suited to their specific contexts. Information services departments (including learning technology units), with their knowledge of technology and its potential future role in universities, are well placed to help facilitate the change process, but need to be supported and empowered by their institutions to do so in a deep and thorough way.

References

Centre for Educational Technology Interoperability Standards (2004) www.cetis.ac.uk.

Checkland, P. (1999) *Systems Thinking, Systems Practice: includes a 30-year retrospective*, Chichester, J. Wiley & Sons Ltd.

Espejo, R., Bowling, D. and Hoverstadt, P. (1999) The Viable System Model and the Viplan Software, *Kybernetes*, **28** (6/7), 661–78.

Holyfield, S. E. and Liber, O. (1995) Using the WWW for the Management of Online Resources, *Active Learning*, **2**, 30–3.

Joint Information Systems Committee (2004a) Exchange for Learning Programme, www.jisc.ac.uk/index.cfm?name=programme_x4l.

Joint Information Systems Committee (2004b) JISC E-Learning Programme, www.jisc.ac.uk/index.cfm?name=programme_elearning.

Joint Information Systems Committee (2004c) Managed Learning Environments, www.jisc.ac.uk/index.cfm?name=mle_home.

JORUM (2004) The JISC Online Repository for [Learning and Teaching] Materials, www.jorum.ac.uk/.

Liber, O. and Holyfield, S. E. (eds) (2003) 'Creating an MLE' infokit, www.jiscinfonet.ac.uk/InfoKits/creating-an-mle.

Mumford, E. (1995) *Effective Systems Design and Requirements Analysis: the ETHICS approach*, Basingstoke, Macmillan.

RELOAD (2004) Reusable Learning Object Authoring and Delivery project, www.reload.ac.uk.

SAKAI (2004) Sakai Project, www.sakaiproject.org.

TOIA (2004) Tools for Online Interoperable Assessment, www.toia.ac.uk.

3

Change management

Robert Hunter, Stephen Clarke, Michele Shoebridge

Introduction

The rapidly developing use of e-learning is changing the role and culture of library and information services. Not only is it placing additional requirements on central support services, but directors of central support services are becoming influential and powerful decision makers at the heart of the strategic planning processes. This presents institutions with multiple challenges: senior managers need to take a proactive and formative role in the formulation of appropriate institutional strategy, develop and implement service delivery systems for an e-learning environment and ensure a shift in culture so that all their staff are able to support the use of this service fully. In some institutions the responsibility for the provision of the e-learning service is a natural part of the remit for library and information services. This requires not only effective change management, but also development of a range of new skills and the bringing together of specialists from previously disparate fields.

This chapter considers the high-level strategic issues that should be addressed as part of the process to develop and implement an e-learning environment, including the skills profile of the service. It looks at ways in which the sector as a whole is supporting, and benefiting from, e-learning.

Background

E-learning now represents a significant proportion of learning and teaching activity in most colleges and universities. E-learning manifests itself in a number of ways, in most cases universities and colleges focus their e-learning activity upon the use of virtual learning environments (VLEs) or managed learning environments (MLEs). The use of these two terms is discussed by the Joint Information Systems Committee (JISC) Briefing Paper 01 (2002). In the context of this chapter the two terms can be considered interchangeable. As the use of VLEs and e-learning in general continues to grow so the need for institutional strategies for the support and development of e-learning becomes more evident, as supported by the findings of the JISC Study of MLE Activity (JISC, 2003), which concluded that:

> The two most common strategic models for managing MLE development within the institution are now 'predominantly centrally managed activity' (40% of responding institutions); and an institution-wide initiative with responsibilities devolved to departments and units within the institution (27%). This indicates a significant move towards more strategic developments.

In many institutions, central library, information and learning support services are leading the provision of e-learning services. According to the Universities and Colleges Information Systems Association (UCISA) survey of July 2003, in 85% of higher education institutions (HEIs) the central IT services provide and support the VLE. This provides senior managers in library and information services (LIS) with a considerable strategic challenge. This chapter focuses on managing the change process necessary to respond to that challenge and looks at developing and implementing a strategy for e-learning. The issues covered include how changes occur, acquiring and implementing support for a VLE, the need for new skills for LIS staff, building effective teams, reviewing staffing structures and a model to underpin the pedagogy for e-learning.

A vision for e-learning

In the early days the use of information and communications technologies (ICT) for learning and teaching focused on the development of learning materials, with a wide range of initiatives that go back to the 1960s, and possibly earlier. One of the largest initiatives in the 1990s was the Teaching and Learning Technology Programme (TLTP, n.d.) funded by the higher education funding councils. Many valuable lessons were learnt from TLTP, in particular the need to embed learning materials into the mainstream curriculum. This embedding became a part of the third phase of TLTP. Other initiatives such as the Fund for the Development of Teaching and Learning (FDTL, n.d.) have also focused on embedding innovative learning and teaching into the mainstream curriculum. Many of the FDTL innovations involve learning technologies – but they put students at the centre, helping them to become more responsible for their own learning.

One of the key issues around using learning technologies to support student-centred learning was raised in the MacFarlane Report (CSUP, 1992). MacFarlane had a vision of an ISLE, an intensely supported learning environment, where learners were provided with a wide range of support using a range of learning technologies. The Dearing Report (NCIHE, 1997) highlights the importance of ICT and learning technologies in the creation of a learning society, in response, MacFarlane (1998) argues that more needs to be done to create a learning society and that it would require 'a fundamental change in the attitude of society to learning and knowledge'. In short he argues that it is not how much we use the technology, more a question of how. MacFarlane's vision of an ISLE, with ICT enabling the fundamental change in how we support a learning society, is now becoming much more of a reality as the technology develops. Perhaps we can work towards what MacFarlane might call an intensely supported learning *society*.

The current position – where are we now?

Less than five years ago e-learning might have been considered the preserve of 'specialists' and 'enthusiasts'. While these early adopters were well respected and influential, e-learning was not seen as part of the mainstream. Many people considered that e-learning was 'not for them', or just too difficult and time consuming. Thanks to the persistence and vision of the early adopters, e-learning is now very much coming of age with many academics using what has become known as 'blended learning', a mix of e-learning with traditional learning and teaching methods. The JISC (2003) study showed that, as of the survey date of March 2003, 83% of respondents were using VLEs. Other evidence, such as the UCISA survey in July 2003 which showed 86% of institutions using a VLE, would suggest that that figure is still rising and there are new models of e-learning developing (Twig, 2003).

The way in which VLEs are used varies from those institutions that are still in the pilot phase, with perhaps more than one VLE being assessed and a small percentage of courses online, to those with institution-wide implementations. Some institutions will have over 70% of students accessing online learning content, making VLEs mission critical to the core business of learning and teaching. Not only do current VLEs provide support for a high proportion of students, but they also support a range of learning styles and activities. A few examples of different course styles include; delivery of text, images and assessments; problem-based learning; scaffold learning (based on moderated discussion groups); interactive video analysis; and trial and improvement with formative assessments.

VLEs can also support generic and transferable skills, such as ICT and information skills, personal development planning and staff development. In many successful cases e-learning is used to develop precisely the skills that staff need to make better use of e-learning in their own teaching, such as the 20 credit 'Certificate in E-learning in Higher Education' available to all teaching and support staff at the University of Birmingham (see www.ldu.bham.ac.uk).

The near future – where are we going?

The range of learning styles that can be supported by VLEs shows that they are becoming increasingly sophisticated, but they still have considerable development potential. As these technologies mature they will enable educational institutions to develop further innovative ways of learning and teaching and will help to change how learning and teaching processes are managed. As VLEs become institutional services, or 'academic enterprise systems', the services on offer can be combined into a single 'portalized' interface, considerably enhancing learning support and management. Web interfaces for library catalogues, student management systems and finance systems are bringing a range of previously remote systems directly onto users' desktops. As these systems increasingly share and exchange information the potential is considerable.

It would appear that the general shift within society towards 'personalization' will become the norm within higher education. Portalization will be a key technique for delivering a personalized view of learning. By using the Institutional VLE (iVLE) and other services from the portalized landscape, learners will be able to put together programmes of study specifically tailored to their own learning needs. Learners will have access to a range of learning opportunities on campus, at home, in the workplace or in a local access centre such as a library or learning centre, enabling them to personalize their own 'e-learning space' and so making the most effective use of the wide range of resources and technologies that are available. These developments support MacFarlane's (1998) view that e-learning technologies will fundamentally change how learning is supported and managed. This implies a modified, but not lessened role for higher education in general, and library and information services in particular.

Personalization of learning, however, is not a random process and although it is centred around the learner it will not diminish the role of educationalists. A range of expertise, most of it already widely used, will still be required to create learning opportunities. Information professionals, instructional designers, subject experts, will still support, guide and teach learners, so researchers, tutors and traditional support roles will still be essential. In fact, the people supporting the learning society will be, for the most part, the same people who are supporting current learning programmes. However, the way in which those people do their work, and in particular the way they interact with each other in their 'communities of practice', is likely to change. In many institutions changes are already happening, and indeed the changes needed are perhaps less radical and disruptive than might be expected. Central services in general, and LIS services in particular, have an opportunity to be active in the change process.

As explored in more detail later in the chapter, effective use of a VLE requires a wide range of support services including IT support, database management, staff development, learning support and development and library services. The 2003 UCISA survey gives a raft of statistics that show that in the majority of cases these services are provided by centrally managed teams, for example 85% of VLEs are supported by central IT teams and 57% of institutions with a VLE are using it to help deliver some of their information resources (UCISA, 2003). Precisely which parts of the support infrastructure fall within the overall LIS remit will vary between institutions, but in all institutions there will be a substantial involvement. So the role of LIS is central in leading the changes necessary to support e-learning, and thereby in ensuring that existing institutions are able to play a full and active part in the new learning society.

The changes that e-learning will inevitably bring about may be perceived as a threat to the traditional strengths of an institution and members of the institution may find it difficult to see their place in the new learning society. While learning technologies will undoubtedly have a significant effect on how and when we learn, in the future there will still be schools, colleges and universities with real campuses and real libraries. Learners will still want to socialize with other learners and with their tutors and to engage in extracurricular activities.

The University of the Highlands and Islands (www.uhi.ac.uk) is an example of a university that sees itself as 'in no way a virtual university'

– (www.uhi.ac.uk/courses/why_uhi/intro_UHI.htm). In fact it is a very real university 'with real buildings staffed by real people'. Nevertheless this university maintains its presence and identity with the help of substantial investment in technology. Other educational establishments will have new opportunities to enhance what they are doing within their traditional boundaries and to develop outside their traditional boundaries. Outward looking institutions can establish their presence in schools, shops, offices, factories and local communities. A good example of this can be seen in Monash University (www.monash.edu.au/about/glance.html), established on the outskirts of Melbourne in 1958. Monash University now has a presence in Italy, London, South Africa and Malaysia. The university makes extensive use of technology and 'increasingly locates its operations, both physically and virtually, around the World' (www.monash.edu.au/international/globaldevelopment/index2.html). Virtual learning and teaching can also enhance recruitment to more traditional campus-based courses. A good example of this can be seen in the blended 'Access to Birmingham' course (www.marketing.bham. ac.uk/recruitment/access.htm), a ten credit course that will support pupils' applications and extend their learning environment beyond school, and offer students, traditional and non-traditional, the opportunity to enhance their qualifications and improve their chances of gaining a full degree place.

Already we can see that right across the sector the learning environment is extending. For most learners the extended learning environment, and the learning within it, will be formal and informal. MacFarlane (1998) predicts a big growth in the demand for learning, as e-learning increases the opportunities for learning in general. E-learning will enable us to drop in and out of learning as and when we want, and LIS will need to be able to support these new types of learners alongside the existing learners. Many LIS departments are already recognizing this, giving non-traditional learners access to books, journals and computing facilities with national initiatives such as the 'Inspire Project' (www.inspire.gov.uk/), 'UK Libraries Plus' and 'UK Computing Plus' (www.uklibrariesplus.ac.uk), alongside many local and bilateral agreements.

Developing a strategy

How do we change?

One of the most positive things that we can see around us is that library, information and other support services are responding instinctively, and thereby benefiting from ICT in general and e-learning in particular. This is clear from the high levels of adoption of centrally supported VLEs and the extension of professional development and support programmes. The UCISA survey (2003) shows that in nearly three-quarters of institutions 'VLEs are widely recognised as an important component of an institutional strategy, but this is yet poorly matched by delivery'. Turning expertise and instinct into strategy can help to match the delivery to the aspirations. Many institutions, 47% according to the JISC (2003) study, are already taking opportunities to do this through input to institutional strategies such as e-learning strategies, learning, teaching and assessment strategies, information management strategies and LIS services' own strategic plans. Frequently the main strategic responsibility for developing e-learning is landing directly on the desks of the directors of LIS or their equivalent.

We know that there is currently 'considerable variation in the level and style of support for e-learning' (JISC, 2003). Several institutions are developing robust infrastructures to support it. Those that are well advanced need to ensure that e-learning goes beyond the technology, so that it is truly learner focused. Visiting the websites of LIS departments shows how diverse they are in terms of their structures. Considering this diversity, and the wide range of skills that are required to develop and implement e-learning, suggests that there is no single solution for implementing e-learning support.

Although there has been much written on change management in this and similar contexts, there is relatively little on how to put theory into practice. One project that attempts to do this is the 'Impact on People of Electronic Libraries' project (IMPEL2, 1998). IMPEL2 looked at the impact of ICT on the teaching, learning and research activities of academic libraries in higher education and highlights the fact that no one institutional structure fits all. Structures must take into account key factors especially the 'political, cultural and historical factors'. The study also recognizes that many institutions have converged but that:

> organisational convergence of Library and Computing Services is not an automatic guarantee of closer working relations although a number of factors will contribute:
>
> - Convergence of operations as services continue to overlap
> - Horizontal and vertical communication
> - Joint staff development and training
> - Training and management support for staff involved in change
> - Key post holders acting as change agents
> - Leadership and clear direction
> - IT and Information Strategies linked to institutional strategic goals.
>
> (IMPEL2, 2000)

With these components in place, clear direction from the service director and an effective senior management team, a converged service (one that brings together library, IT and often other central support services) is well positioned to succeed in implementing change. Those institutions that need to co-ordinate the work of a number of different departments will face an additional challenge. No matter what is currently in place, implementing e-learning will require change, and effective management of that change will be an important success factor. The Chartered Institute of Library and Information Professionals (CILIP) recognizes the wide variations in how libraries are managed and that managing change is always complex. No single model fits all, so CILIP commissioned the Change Management Toolkit (CILIP, 2003). This toolkit is intended to provide 'ideas, insights, and lines of thought; tools to help you think through different approaches and to apply key principles to your own situation. It will support you as you work through the elements in the process of change'.

The toolkit focuses on five key areas:

- the nature and scope of the change
- the main elements in successful change management
- the nature of your organization – how will it cope with change?
- key factors to support or hinder change
- working with people – the personal dimension of change.

Although the Change Management Toolkit was developed to implement the Peoples' Network it can be adapted for implementing e-learning, no matter what type of infrastructures are in place. However, as highlighted by the IMPEL2 report, change management also involves the development and implementation of strategy: without a strategy there is no direction. The IMPEL2 report suggests that an information strategy should 'coordinate the efforts of all parts of the structure' and should involve:

- An open atmosphere which encourages consultation, communication and innovation
- Clear links between institutional mission, strategy and organizational structures
- A committed Strategy Panel with balanced membership including academics, institutional managers and Heads of service departments
- Avoidance of aggressive politics
- Thorough analysis of the external and internal environments
- Greater emphasis on the needs of the internal community than on technology
- Appreciation of the potential and implications of IT in all its forms for the institution
- Recognition that LIS and Computing Services are as central to the core business of HE as academic teaching

- Recognition that questions of IT skills are strategic issues for the institution
- Balanced content between Library, Academic and Administrative computing
- Avoidance of platitudinous wording.

(IMPEL2, 2000)

Developing structures to support e-learning

A key part of the strategy for e-learning is to develop robust support structures. From a central service perspective, the e-learning service will consist of software, technical support, user support and management structures to ensure that the service continues to develop and respond to users' needs. These needs are inherently difficult to determine. In an area where there will be many differing opinions and little or no objective evidence, there is likely to be considerable debate. In order to focus that discussion and debate there are three initial strategic questions that need to be answered.

1 *Is a VLE the best solution?* The JISC and UCISA surveys showed that over 80% of institutions were already using one or more VLEs with the proportion continuing to increase. Clearly the majority view is that a VLE is a useful resource to support learning and teaching. How well a VLE works in any particular institution will depend on how it is implemented.
2 *Should a single VLE be deployed or a range of VLEs?* Providing a range of VLEs will give a choice of e-learning platforms. On the other hand supporting more than one VLE will dilute effort and expertise; it also leads to a wider distribution of learning materials, rather than a 'one stop shop for all learning' (JISC, 2003). The industry publication *Computing* has run a series of recent articles on UK HEIs that are seeing extensive growth in the use of e-learning, comments such as 'Over the past year, the level of usage has more than doubled and we expect the same to happen over the next 12 months' (Mortleman, 2004) are commonplace. In

each of the cases cited the institution has a policy of supporting a single institutional VLE.

3 *Should the VLE be home grown, open source or commercial?* A typical commercial vendor will already have had a large development team working on the product for some years. A small team of ten developers working for five years will have already spent around 100,000 hours on product development alone, not to mention the associated activities such as user consultation and documentation. So unless that level of resource can be made available, a home-grown solution is not going to match the commercial products for functionality and performance. Open source – defined by the *Free On-line Dictionary of Computing* (FOLDOC) as 'A method and philosophy for software licensing and distribution designed to encourage use and improvement of software written by volunteers by ensuring that anyone can copy the source code and modify it freely' – can seem attractive as there are no licensing costs. However, there are other costs, such as product support and development, that form part of the total cost of ownership. The drawback of commercial solutions is the licence fee, but when considered within the overall e-learning budget, licence fees are not the main cost, and in return for the licence fee customers should receive a proven product that is well documented, well supported and for which there is a widespread pool of expertise. In reality the pragmatic solution is likely to include elements of all three options. Commercial systems may need custom-built integrations and home-grown or open-source systems may be built and extended with commercial tools. All three approaches have their place, but having a clear strategic steer on the preferred direction can save considerable time and effort.

The next part of the strategy is to map out the staff and skill sets needed to implement, support and embed use of e-learning. The necessary support systems and services need to be planned. These will be determined by the departmental structures and the political, cultural and historical factors. A helpful way of planning an e-learning service is to divide it into a series of layers (see Figure 3.1) showing the aspects of the service and the staff involved. The different layers are described below.

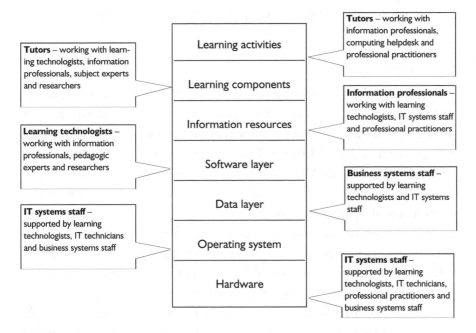

Figure 3.1 Support layers of an e-learning service

Learning activities

The students' primary reason for using the VLE is the learning activities. These are managed primarily by tutors, lecturers, teachers, instructors and so on. However, library-based information professionals, professional practitioners, mentors and postgraduate students can also be involved.

Learning components

To create learning activities, the tutors will need to aggregate a range of learning components. These can include text, diagrams or simulations, and facilities to support activities, such as discussion boards, assessment tools or any other facilities that can contribute to learning. Tutors are the primary managers of this layer, but need help, guidance and support from other professionals in creating and compiling the learning components. The staff involved include, but are not restricted to, instructional designers, learning technologists, information professionals, subject experts and researchers.

Information resources

To facilitate the embedding of information resources, for instance online textbooks, datasets, e-journals, into learning content there is an organized suite of resource discovery and retrieval tools, sometimes referred to as a digital library. This layer may have an existence in its own right outside the VLE, but the information professionals are the best group to design the service so that tutors are aware of the e-resources that are available to them. This approach will help tutors to embed high quality e-resources into programmes of study. A well designed information resources service should reduce the trend for tutors and students to use less reliable internet resources (Brophy, 2002).

Technically there is a range of issues with integrating digital learning resources into VLEs, and institutions are working with the system vendors to address them. To support effective use of the technology that exists now, and that will be developed in the near future, all the key stakeholders, especially academics, can make valuable contributions in helping to select resources and reviewing the ways in which resources can be embedded. The better the quality of the resources that are available to academics, the more successful the integration with the VLE will be. Failing to make electronic learning resources available with the VLE may create unnecessary barriers to learning and could undermine the effectiveness of the overall service.

Software layer

Underpinning the content and information resource layers is a software layer. This is the programme or system that helps to create, manage and present the learning components. This layer is usually managed by learning technologists, with technical and pedagogic knowledge, skills and experience. This is a critical layer and the learning technologists can better achieve their objectives by forming a close working relationship with tutors, knowledge managers and other learning support staff, in order to understand and interpret their needs. The learning technologists will also benefit from being able to call on support from database specialists – to manage the data layer and IT systems staff, who will manage the hardware and operating systems.

Data layer

The database specialists will have primary responsibility for the data management, but will work closely with, and be guided by, the learning technologists and the IT systems staff.

Operating system

Managing the operating system for a large-scale file server, as will be required for any VLE platform, is an expert job. The software application, the size of the implementation and the level of usage will determine the configuration. That configuration will change as the system grows and develops, as will the requirements for backing-up, upgrading and security. Specialist IT systems staff are best qualified to take a lead in this area, but the system must also accommodate the needs of the learning technologists and the integration and interactions with other systems – particularly the business process systems such as staffing and student records. Also important within the team supporting the operating system will be the technicians who may diagnose problems, perform back-ups and carry out other maintenance tasks.

Hardware

Like the operating system, understanding, specifying, configuring and supporting the hardware for a system of this scale is complex and specialized. The lead will naturally be taken by people with an authoritative knowledge and understanding of hardware. As with all other parts of the support structure, these people will work closely with, and be guided by, the other stakeholders and make maximum use of existing people and processes.

Overseeing the process

To oversee the whole process, there may be benefits in having a single accountable person with ultimate responsibility for ensuring that the parts fit together. In many places this role is now being referred to as 'Head of E-learning', although many other titles can describe the same role. The national Heads of e-Learning Forum, or HeLF (www.helf.ac.uk), already has a single nominated member from two-thirds of the UK HEIs, with more institutions joining. The head of e-learning may have direct management responsibility for one or more of the components, but has a co-ordinating role across the institution.

The model shown in Figure 3.1 is generic, and there are many ways in which responsibilities can be shared and divided. The benefit of identifying the layers in this way is that it helps to decide who needs to do what, and more importantly who is responsible for what. This approach can also provide a useful vehicle for agreeing and sharing the vision for e-learning. Going through this process and using it to help develop a strategy will probably involve contact with other parts of the institution, and it is therefore essential to develop a strategy that feeds into other relevant strategy papers such as the learning, teaching and assessment strategy, LIS strategy, the mission statement and overall strategy of the institution. Following the IMPEL2 guidelines outlined above will facilitate the development of a strategy that has a shared ownership, and which is therefore more likely to be implemented.

Implementing a strategy

When the strategy has been agreed the 'Change Management Toolkit' can be adapted to guide implementation. Also of potential use is

Kotter's paper 'Why Transformation Efforts Fail' (Kotter, 1995). Kotter researched a number of change programmes that had failed and came up with eight steps to success:

1 *Establish a sense of urgency.* Learning technologies are changing the way we do many things; e-learning will significantly change the way we learn and LIS will most likely need to adapt and change.
2 *Form a powerful guiding coalition.* The ideal is to assemble a group that should have enough power and resources to support and enable the change effort. It will also be crucial for this group to work as an effective team.
3 *Create a vision.* The vision will support and direct the change effort. Strategies should be developed for achieving the vision and should be fed into the institutional strategies.
4 *Communicate the vision.* Try and use all available communication channels and, where possible, develop new ones such as newsletters and websites.
5 *Empower others to act on the vision.* Face up to the obstacles for change, as these undermine the vision. For e-learning this will usually involve changes in staff structures, such as the creation of a team of learning technologists, an e-learning team, and the appointment or identification of an appropriate person to take on overall responsibility, for example a head of e-learning. The e-learning team will need to be empowered and given strong leadership in order to develop the support systems. Kotter also suggests that we should encourage risk taking and non-traditional ideas, activities and actions. To do this effectively, a cultural change may be required. If staff are going to be empowered then managed risk taking should be supported, avoiding blame, and systems should be put in place to evaluate how effective change has been. Highlighting good practice and lessons learnt can help to create a positive feedback cycle and lead to further cultural change.
6 *Plan and create successes.* Have milestones that are part of the change process and recognize and reward staff who are part of these changes.

7 *Consolidate improvements and produce further change.* As the change process develops be careful not to declare success too soon. Building on the improvements should help to remove obstacles. For e-learning this could involve building on good practice in one area that may be suitable for another. Look for added value and unexpected gains, and use these to seed new projects.

8 *Institutionalize new approaches.* Try and make the new approaches the norm by embedding them and aim to show how the changes fit in with and support the institutional strategies.

One of the key factors not covered by Kotter is staff development. The layers identified in Figure 3.1 (page 67) for implementing e-learning define the staff roles. Most of these people will need support and many will need personal skills development. To make the implementation a success ensure that people receive the support and development they need.

Staff development

How learning takes place

A review of the changing nature of work in academic libraries in the United States between 1973 and 1998 'demonstrates that by 1998, all academic library jobs routinely included computer technologies, that instruction had become an integral part of reference work, and that behavioural skills, especially oral and written communication skills, had emerged as new job requirements' (Lynch and Smith, 2001). From this we see that ICT is extending the roles of library service staff, especially in the areas of instruction and learning support. The above study was carried out in 2000 and covered library jobs up to 1998. Since then e-learning has developed significantly and, as the JISC (2003) study of MLE activity shows, the majority of educational institutions are implementing some form of support for e-learning. The Online Computer Library Center, Inc. (OCLC) E-learning Task Force (2003) agreed that 'pedagogy, learning methodologies and technology have become linked and that the interrelationship among these needs to be better understood'.

Blended learning is the most common approach in linking these areas and it is changing staff roles. This trend is highlighted by a plethora of events that focus on e-learning such as the conference held jointly by the Society of College, National and University Libraries (SCONUL) and UCISA 'E-learning: the evolving role of academic services', in 2004. At this conference participants agreed that 'these staff are now fundamental to, and directly engaged in, the learning process, rather than simply passive "supporters" of learners. To design and deliver proactive services and resources in an e-learning environment staff need an understanding of how learning takes place' (Carly, Jolly and Berry, 2004). An enhanced understanding of learning processes is therefore important.

In learning support centres, staff provide for a range of learning activities and, with the ever expanding use of VLEs, the range and style of activities is continuing to grow. Staff involved in academic liaison and support are finding they need to develop pedagogic skills further to advise academic teaching staff best on how to make maximum use of the available learning resources.

Allan (2002) gives useful examples of how some universities now offer courses for academic support staff that will develop their understating of learning. There is also a good review of a range of courses developed through the EFFECTS (Effective Framework for Embedding C and IT using Targeted Support) programme, available at www.elt.ac.uk. These programmes include activities to develop an understanding of how we learn, how to support students online and how to adapt and develop content for online learning. With these skills LIS staff can proactively support academic staff in their use of e-learning.

Developing and supporting effective teams

Another key factor, and one that Kotter does not highlight, is the value of effective teams. Where LIS services incorporate a wide range of support services there will still tend to be teams that focus primarily on technological support, teams that focus on information management and teams that focus on pedagogic support. Where the services are delivered by separate departments the distance between them is likely to be greater, with the departments having separate remits and strategic aspirations. However, whatever level of convergence exists within the central service departments, the challenge is similar: to develop effective horizontal teams.

The development and implementation of e-learning provides an opportunity to develop horizontal working, as e-learning support requires a wide range of skills. There may also be other teams not directly involved in supporting the VLE that should to be involved. Each team needs clear aims and objectives, with achievable milestones, and must know how their work relates to others. This requires 'a powerful guiding coalition' (Kotter, 1995), perhaps in the form of a steering group. This group will be responsible for implementing the strategy and should be committed to the change process. The membership should have a balance of academic staff, institutional managers, heads of service departments and other key stakeholders. The guiding coalition will enable implementation to go ahead, but will not be the implementer. To achieve effective implementation the guiding coalition must work together to build effective teams. Developing e-learning requires a variety of teams. Some teams will become a permanent part of the management structure while others will carry out a specific set of tasks.

Successful teams should have:

- *Objectives.* These should be clear, achievable, regularly monitored and must form part of a higher level strategy.
- *Project management methodology.* This should be supportive, easily understood, and have consistent documentation and working practices.
- *Resources.* These should be allocated correctly. There should be sufficient but not excessive resource. If the balance is wrong either way then there is too much pressure on the team.

- *Support and professional development.* Staff may require basic skills development to work in teams, such as time management, but the most important are interpersonal qualities such as negotiating and influencing skills.

It may be easier to create effective teams in a converged service, because a greater proportion of the necessary staff will report into a single central service director. In the model put forward in Figure 3.1 (page 67) it can be seen that, apart from academic teaching staff, all the staff would usually be part of a converged service. Where a converged service is not in place there has to be a clear strategy that is owned by the different services, backed-up by a collaborative working culture. Project teams promote these horizontal links, both within converged services and across other central services.

Staff involved in implementing an e-learning strategy will often automatically become agents of change as people are faced with alterations to the way they do their work. One example of this occurred during the Information Services Change Management Programme at the University of Birmingham (Shoebridge, 2004), where staff previously involved in cataloguing printed and electronic materials moved into new roles as 'learning advisors' and 'subject consultants'. In these new roles the staff needed to acquire skills to support blended learning, in particular for the development of subject-specific learning resources. The academic liaison role is also key in supporting blended learning; staff involved in this area can benefit from being ambitious in developing their pedagogical skills well beyond the traditional level and thereby become active members of curriculum development teams.

Successful change management requires a demonstrable commitment to staff development. Strategic documents outlining the staff development policy are useful, especially if supported by an action plan with a clear representation of the training and development taking place. Effective team and individual training plans linked to the staff development review process, personal workbooks and targeted training for specific teams are all helpful techniques. Evaluation of staff development is difficult, but helpful in guiding the development strategy.

Cultivating communities of practice

All organizations have what Wenger (1998) defines as 'communities of practice', which play a key role in sharing and disseminating knowledge. They are informal, with participants self-selecting through a common interest. Communities of practice in e-learning could include senior managers, academic staff, learning technologists, library staff and administrative staff, all sharing an interest in the use of e-learning to support learning and teaching. The important point that Wenger makes is that a community of practice is 'different from a team in that the shared learning and interest of its members are what keep it together. It is defined by knowledge rather than by task and exists because participation has value to its members' (Wenger, 1998).

Wenger argues that communities of practice are essential for knowledge management, which is far more than developing and maintaining databases. Wenger, McDermott and Snyder (2002) see communities of practice as 'the ideal social structure for stewarding knowledge'. For Wenger social interaction is the key to transforming knowledge into practical solutions. Communities of practice are informal, so they need to be encouraged and supported. *A Guide to Managing Knowledge: cultivating communities of practice* by Wenger, McDermott and Snyder (2002), gives pragmatic advice on nurturing these communities of practice and an overview of how the social interaction within the communities of practice ensures dissemination of knowledge.

The Learning Development Unit (LDU) Project Leaders Group at the University of Birmingham gives a good example of an emerging community of practice, with a common interest in using learning technologies to enhance learning. The LDU funds a wide range of projects using learning technologies to develop innovative teaching and learning. Each project has its own formal team structure, with a project leader based in a school or central service department. The

LDU Project Leaders Group provides an informal community of practice that meets face to face and supplements these meetings with an interactive website to share good practice and lessons learnt. This informal community is highly stable with project leaders and members of project teams participating beyond the formal part of their projects. As e-learning continues to grow other members are joining, including library staff, members of the e-learning team and other support staff. This community of practice can also give well informed and authoritative feedback on what changes are required to support e-learning at an institutional level. So far this community of practice has contributed to the development of computer-based collaborative working areas, the upgrade of the institutional VLE and the development of flexible learning spaces. Another outcome from this community of practice has been the development of localized school- and department-based communities of practice all sharing a common interest in e-learning.

Putting it all together

Staffing structures

All the developments outlined above need to be brought together to ensure that e-learning genuinely enhances learning. MacFarlane's (CSUP, 1992) concept of an ISLE, the intensely supported learning environment, referred to earlier in this chapter, is pivotal to enhancing the learning experience for all students and the ISLE will require the appropriate staffing structures and a robust pedagogical underpinning. The VLE is an important and widespread pedagogic tool in HE and FE (JISC, 2003), which is at the core of the ISLE, with different institutions using them in different ways. At one end of the spectrum is what could be called the business systems approach, where the VLE is linked to the management systems of the institution. These links tend to give access to course information, similar to that given in a course booklet. This gives all students some content on the VLE; academics can then add learning resources, activities and support to this content. With this approach there is likely be a central support team to help academics develop content and to provide technical and pedagogic training.

At the other end of the spectrum are models where there is no central support and faculties or departments provide their own support services. With this model the VLE will most likely be managed by the department or faculty, and the academics will either work on their own or have departmental support staff. Somewhere in the middle are models that are based on converged departments. At the University of Birmingham, the Head of E-learning and the E-learning Team are based within the converged department of Information Services. They provide a wide range of support to the academic schools and central services in the use of the VLE and other learning technologies; see Figure 3.2 and www.weblearn.bham.ac.uk for more details.

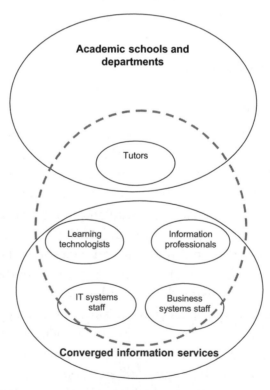

Figure 3.2   E-learning support at the University of Birmingham

The main focus of this support is to enable academic schools and central services to embed the use of e-learning into their own staffing structures and workflow processes, while at the same time ensuring they make the most effective use of the wide range of services that Information Services provide. Key to the success of this approach are the horizontal working relationships with the e-learning team, information professionals, IT and business systems staff. The trend in many other institutions appears to be similar to this model (Cattermole, 2003). However, each institution is different and there are many pragmatic versions being applied. Most institutions are developing staffing structures to embed the use of e-learning into the curriculum.

The underpinning pedagogy

With all these systems in place how can the development of e-learning courses or programmes be supported? Oliver (2002) suggests a very simple model that academics and LIS staff can use to support all aspects of e-learning. It has three elements:

1 'Learning activities – the tasks, problems and interactions used to involve learners and upon which learning is based.' Many LIS staff are now engaging students in a range of learning activities by using the blended approach to learning, to develop students' information skills. As information professionals develop their pedagogical skills they will be better equipped to contribute to curriculum development. At the University of Birmingham information professionals are part of what are now called 'integrated professional teams' working with academics and learning technologists on e-learning projects.
2 'Learning resources – the learning content and information resources with which learners interact during learning activities.' This is an area where LIS staff can have substantial input into curriculum planning, integrating learning resources, learner support and the learning activities with the VLE. Where learning resources

are developed without this integration, they will not be used in the most effective way (DIVLE, 2003). As information professionals engage more in curriculum development, the learning resources for which they are responsible will be used more effectively.

3 'Learner supports – the structures, motivations, assistances and connections that support learning.' As VLEs become more widespread information professionals are becoming more involved in the wider aspects of supporting learners. Many institutions now have learning spaces or learning cafés that are supported by a range of LIS staff. The users of these facilities are engaging in learning activities, so the learner support is not confined to the traditional areas such as technical skills and information skills training. Some institutions have what are termed 'learning advisors' who provide face to face and online learner support. Where this works well it is, in effect, creating an ISLE. Hunter (1997) describes how learning advisors at the University of Lincolnshire and Humberside played a key role in putting together a range of learning activities and learning resources to develop generic skills for students. Using what we would now call a VLE, these learning advisors also provided learner support and are active members of course design committees.

Conclusion

There are many different approaches to developing and supporting e-learning and the choice depends on the local situation and what is appropriate for individual institutions. The key areas for successful implementation are: technical and staff infrastructure; effective teams, both project based and those that develop naturally to form communities of practice; change in the underlying pedagogy; and the cultural change of LIS staff brought about by appropriate and timely staff development.

E-learning is still in the early stages of development but is beginning to have an impact on the mission of most HE institutions. In its widest interpretation it will underpin the move to the personalization of services (SCONUL, 2004) by enabling individuals to create their own learning space or 'learning portal', which will include learning activities, learning logs, continual professional development programmes, learning resources and contacts to support the lifelong learner. This learning space will support individuals through all their 'learning ages' and facilitate the move to an 'intensely supported learning society'. Equally, this move will demand a radical cultural shift among LIS staff if they are going to remain central to the learning process.

References

Allan, B. (2002) *E-learning and Teaching in Library and Information Services*, London, Facet Publishing.

Brophy, P. (2002) Strategic Issues for Academic Libraries, *Relay: the Journal of the University College and Research Group*, **52**, 4–5.

Carly, W. J., Jolly, E. C. and Berry, J. (2004) unpublished report on the SCONUL–UCISA conference *E-learning: the evolving role of academic services*, held 20 January 2004 at the European Research Institute, University of Birmingham.

Cattermole, J. (2003) *Managing in a Converged Service: some considerations from Middlesex University*, Belgrade, Serbian Academic Library Association, Belgrade, www.unilib.bg.ac.yu/en/e-sources/infotheca/1-2003/cattermole1.php.

Chartered Institute of Library and Information Professionals (2003) *Managing Change Tool Kit*, www.cilip.org.uk/practice/managingchange.html.

Committee of Scottish University Principals (1992) *Teaching and Learning in an Expanding Higher Education System*, the MacFarlane Report, Edinburgh, Committee of Scottish University Principals.

DiVLE (2003) *Linking Digital Libraries with VLEs (DiVLE) Programme*, Theme C final report, www.jisc.ac.uk/mle_divle_final_reports.html.

Free On-line Dictionary of Computing (2004)
    http://wombat.doc.ic.ac.uk/foldoc.
Fund for the Development of Teaching and Learning (FDTL),
    www.ncteam.ac.uk/projects/fdtl.
Hunter, R. (1997) The Role of Learning Support in the
    Development of a Key Skills Programme and an Intranet to
    Support it, *Electronic Library*, **15** (5), 357–62.
IMPEL2 Project (1998) *Monitoring Organisational and Cultural
    Change*,
    http://online.northumbria.ac.uk/faculties/art/information_
    studies/impel.
IMPEL2 Project (2000) *Structure and Strategy*,
    http://online.northumbria.ac.uk/faculties/art/information_
    studies/impel/struct.htm.
Joint Information Systems Committee (2002) Briefings Paper 01,
    www.jisc.ac.uk/index.cfm?name=mle_briefings_1.
Joint Information Systems Committee (2003) *Study of MLE
    Activity*, www.jisc.ac.uk/project_mle_activity.html.
Kotter, J. P. (1995) Why Transformation Efforts Fail, *Harvard
    Business Review*, March–April, 59–67.
Lynch, B. P. and Smith, K. R. (2001) The Changing Nature of
    Work in Academic Libraries, *College & Research Libraries*, **62**
    (5), 407–20.
MacFarlane, A. (1998), Information, Knowledge and Learning,
    Higher Education Quarterly, **52** (1), 77–92.
Mortleman, J. (2004) www.vnunet.com/news/1155818;
    www.vnunet.com/news/1156533;
    www.vnunet.com/news/1152670;
    www.vnunet.com/news/1154020.
National Committee of Inquiry into Higher Education (1997)
    Higher Education in the Learning Society (the Dearing Report),
    London, HMSO, www.leeds.ac.uk/educol/ncihe.
Oliver, R. (2002) Winning the Toss and Electing to Bat:
    maximising the opportunities of online learning. In Rust, C.
    (ed.), *Proceedings of the 9th Improving Student Learning*

Conference, Oxford, Oxford Centre for Staff and Learning
Development, 35–44.

Online Computer Library Center E-learning (2003) *Libraries and
the Enhancement of E-learning*, OCLC,
www.oclc.org/index/elearning/default.htm.

Shoebridge, M. I. (2004) Presentation at the SCONUL–UCISA
conference *E-learning: the evolving role of academic services*,
held 20 January 2004 at the European Research Institute,
University of Birmingham.

Society of College, National and University Libraries (2004)
Vision, www.sconul.ac.uk.

Teaching and Learning Technology Programme (TLTP),
www.ncteam.ac.uk/projects/tltp.

Twig, C. A. (2003) *Improving Learning and Reducing Costs: new
models for online learning*,
www.educause.edu/ir/library/pdf/ERM0352.pdf.

Universities and Colleges Information Systems Association (2003)
VLE Survey, www.ucisa.ac.uk/groups/tlig/vle/index_html.

Wenger, E., McDermott, R. and Snyder, W. M. (2002) *A Guide to
Managing Knowledge: cultivating communities of practice,*
Boston, MA, Harvard Business School Press.

Wenger, E. (1998) Communities of Practice: learning as a social
system, *Systems Thinker*, www.co-i-l.com/coil/knowledge-
garden/cop/lss.shtml.

4

Support in the use of new media

Frank Moretti

Introduction

The following comments are addressed to those who are trying to extend the purposeful use of digital technologies within university learning environments. The views expressed represent a distillation of what the author has learned as the Executive Director of the Columbia Center for New Media Teaching and Learning of Columbia University (CCNMTL, http://ccnmtl.columbia.edu). The comments range from the theoretical to the strategic and very practical. The author is aware that to cover so much terrain in so few pages creates a danger but the decision was made to provide a landscape view that will be useful to both the manager and frontline provider of service.

CCNMTL came into existence in 1999 as a response to the recommendations of a university-wide faculty and administration committee charged to look at the state of digital technology on the campus. The committee made a number of recommendations but the first was to create an organization that would have as its mission the service and support of faculty members in their use of digital technologies in the University's matriculated degree programmes. CCNMTL's original staff of three has grown to 30. In its short history it has provided service to over 2000 faculty members with projects ranging from simple course management support to over 150 larger projects, see http://ccnmtl.columbia.edu/projects/. The Center, funded in large part through the University's operating budget, has received over US$5 million in grants and US$10 million in gifts.

Service as invention

Knowing clearly what you are trying to become as an organization is prerequisite to successfully becoming it. This may seem obvious but needs to be consciously in view at a time of rapid change. Institutional arrangements and the language used to describe them are being challenged and reinvented as digital technologies evolve and make new modalities of communication and engagement possible. This is especially the case as one tries to define and manage organizations for which there are no historical antecedents. For instance, if one were to call CCNMTL a specialist support and service unit (and we do), it would not be absurd to assume that what it supports and serves is known in type and character, that it has a stable and universal identity. In fact, the process of 'supporting and serving' in the digital age frequently includes a fundamental reconstruction of the enterprise of teaching and learning itself. If one is to call it a service, therefore, then we must call it a service carefully defined as a proactive effort to attract faculty into simple and complex partnerships in the interest of inventing new possibilities for teaching and learning. One certain fact: we have barely begun to glimpse the landscape of education as it will be practised in the future, no more than the pedagogues of the Early Renaissance could imagine the institutions of education as they would ultimately be shaped by printing.

Furthermore, just as these times require that new educational technology service organizations act as change agents within the pedagogical landscape, it is equally important they play a similar role within the evolving landscape of organizational relationships. Being a good organizational team player has always carried the implication that what is important is to know your place, especially in the necessarily conservative structures for memorializing knowledge and effecting its transmission. These structures were deemed to have a sacrosanct quality within the hermetic world of print. Within them one lived and worked. Now we know that we must reinvent them. Libraries are no longer libraries or simply places of the book and even what began as the computer support organizations of 20 years ago, boutique at the time, can no longer exist in isolation; they have become essential to the conduct of the business of education. The struggle for organizational clarity and effectiveness continues. We must be active and alive to the possible places of convergence and the reordering of these legacy enterprises, both changing libraries with centuries of history and digital organizations with only decades of habits.

In such an environment attitude becomes paramount. We, the creators of digital service organizations and libraries, must represent a nimbleness and an awareness that our success is found more in creation and novelty than conformity and repetition. The profession must not be chosen for its stability and unchanging character. Rather one must see virtue in and be content with the fact that we are victims of the curse of living in interesting times. We must take pleasure in trying to imagine the possible and seek to create the yet unseen as all part of the process of contributing a new landscape of knowledge, study and learning.

Importance of history: vision and a caution

Before the personal computer's ascendancy and before the conversation in educational circles was hijacked by this last decade's conservatives with their focus on standards and control from the top down, there existed a robust dialogue focused on educational reform, driven by pedagogical and curricular innovation. This extension of the progressive movement was often described as constructivist because of its emphasis on almost any students' capacity to learn by creating their own understandings within an artfully constructed environment. Drawing their inspiration from John Dewey and his successors (and predecessors, Plato and Rousseau) the challenge was to create a curriculum context, elaborate the challenges (questions, projects, and so on) and provide access to the primary source content that defined the field of intellectual endeavour as well as whatever tools students might use to develop responses or solutions.

Enter digital technologies in the 1980s! Some reformers (Alan Kay, Seymour Papert, Don Nix, Robbie McClintock)[1] quickly embraced them as capable of facilitating constructivist learning in new and unique ways. Not only could primary source content of all types (filmic, photos, sound and text) be collated and 'delivered', they could be situated within simulated contexts in which students were given access to tools that allowed a new and unique form of engagement. Archeological simulations, such as Archeotype, situated the work of students, sixth graders of the Dalton School and first-year archeology graduate students at Columbia, in a simulated excavation of an ancient Sumerian city, Til Barsip, with the challenge of 'digging up' the artefacts and re-creating the history and culture. At their disposal in their digital universe, supported by five networked Apple Classics, were measuring and weighing devices, the antiquities collection of the Louvre on interactive videodisc, customized libraries of research resources and a growing archive of the student 'excavation' results that also acted as a place where asynchronous exchange and debate could occur over the identification and meaning of their finds. The revolution was upon us; reformers had found sticks big enough to move the archaic boulder of the stale pedagogies and processes of the didactic past. Universities and schools were to become reinvigorated with the possibilities glimpsed in these early days.

Enter the world wide web! The birth of the information superhighway! Grasping at quick solutions to complex educational dilemmas, encouraged by simplistic politics (a T1 in every pot), and spirited by the commercial sector, which saw the possibility of a low overhead of a 'point–click–purchase' world, educators seemed to almost universally embrace the notion that 'access to information' was a magical incantation that would cure all educational woes for students, young and old. If only everyone could have access to the data, everyone would magically learn! Everyone seemed to forget the lessons of the past and the basic wisdom that education has to do with purposeful activity in which the learner finds their way to new understandings in an artfully constructed environment, whether the programme is math for six year olds or a programme leading to a PhD.

The intellectual and educational insufficiency of an almost exclusive focus on information access has always been understood by the lords of cyber fiction such as Neil Stephenson (1992). Observe how he describes a digital librarian (actually digital) in *Snow Crash*:

> The librarian daemon looks like a pleasant, fiftyish, silver-haired, bearded man with blue eyes, wearing a V-neck sweater over a work shirt, with a coarsely woven, tweedy-looking wool tie. The tie is loosened, the sleeves pushed up. Even though he's just a piece of software, he has reason to be cheerful; he can move through the nearly infinite stacks of information in the Library with the agility of a spider dancing across a vast web of cross references. The Library is the only piece of CIC software that costs more than Earth [software to keep track of every piece of global spatial information in a three dimensional virtual world]; the only thing he can't do is think.

The only thing our cyber-librarian can't do is think. It is just as foolish to expect students to be motivated to think and learn simply by virtue of the presence of information presented in the data mall of the web. The new ubiquity and accessibility of information is a part of what is new and significant, but alone, without attention to context and tools, one is left like our cyber-librarian able to collate, assemble, sort and so on but not to make knowledge and meaning. Certainly the language we have naturally evolved to describe web engagement confirms this. One surfs the web's flickering universe, a most contemporary *flaneur* that makes Benjamin more right than he ever knew.

Only when we begin to realize the power of the technology to provide before unimaginable tools of analysis, visualization and authoring have we begun to glimpse the new horizon of the promised pedagogical revolution. To say this about the technology to an architect or a banker would elicit a quick confirmation because for them technology refers to its capacity to facilitate transactions involving presentation, manipulation and communications. How ironic is it that the argument has to be made to educators! Those most interested in real digital libraries are starting to glimpse the problem: that information as a collectible fungible commodity only becomes a value when situated in a process of meaning making and knowledge construction. McLean and Lynch (2004) in their recent article on libraries and learning begin to identify and struggle with the problem they call 'bridging the gaps':

> There is growing acceptance that simply making resources available on the network without an additional layer of services may not be very effective. There are some clear reasons for this, arising from the characteristics of the current generation of network resources. In general, many of these characteristics flow from the fact that the resources are made available at interfaces with low levels of interconnectedness between them. This in turn puts the burden of interconnection back on the user and it means that the potential value of interconnection is not realized.

McClean and Lynch bravely dip their toes in some new waters by recognizing the inadequacy of just presenting information.[2] They call both for use-scenarios that mobilize engagement and a new library world-view that would eliminate the separation of responsibilities that have become so hard-coded that there is often a sacrosanct chasm between libraries as the keepers of information and the faculty as the keepers of the pedagogical flame. They see the importance of making 'connections' as an essential dimension of learning. Implicit in their analysis is the awareness that learning does not take place through an object that one observes but an action that one takes. It is time for the architects of digital libraries and those interested in inventing the pedagogy of the 21st century to join forces in the invention of our educational future.[3]

Digital service entities can provide motivation for bringing together the traditionally separated activities of information provision and context and tool construction. They must represent the new partnerships made possible by the fact that digital technologies are the common stuff of information in all media forms, of the tools of engagement – editing, analysis, authoring – as well as the use scenarios that provide the context to make students work activity driven and purposeful. Those who build and manage them must focus on the new seamlessness of the pedagogical revolution. They need to recover from the web-induced lapse into naive empiricism that dictates that to get the so-called objects to the learners will magically occasion learning. They must recognize unique opportunities the technologies provide to situate the learner in an active tool context connected to new emerging capacities to configure and present information. They must recognize similar opportunities to construct challenging and interesting use-scenarios. It must become as natural for libraries to suggest tools and context possibilities as it must for service entities to integrate information resources and digital libraries in their constructions. Lines between what were before discrete entities have become blurred and it is necessary to grapple with the creation of their future connections and articulations.

Two vignettes of practice and the rules for engagement

Vignette 1: the development with Professor Herbert Ginsburg, Teachers College, Columbia University, of Video Interactions for Teaching and Learning (VITAL; http://ccnmtl.columbia.edu/projects/feature_pages/168-Vital.pdf)

CCNMTL was approached by Professor Herbert Ginsburg, a professor in the Graduate School of Education, Teachers College, who wanted to know if we could help him. He described himself as having a hunch that digital technologies properly applied could advance his efforts over 20 years to use his video library of clinical interviews of children solving mathematical problems, to teach in-service and pre-service teachers certain basic skills and attitudes related to mathematics education. Professor Ginsburg described himself as carrying stacks of VHS tapes that he used in class to point out the creative and unusual ways that children solve mathematical problems in order to sensitize teachers to the fact that one-size-fits-all pedagogies can often blind one to emerging thought in children. Professor Ginsburg pointed out his frustration that, with a class of 50, students were not able to use the tapes to study nor was he able to evaluate their ability to observe and discriminate behaviours represented in the interview.

CCNMTL began by explaining they could construct a digital library of interviews but asked Professor Ginsburg what did he really want to accomplish? The team quickly realized that Professor Ginsburg would still not be able to assess, even with a digital library, the student level of understanding fully except through their written assignments documented with loose references to the interviews. The team asked the question, what is it that students could be asked to do in an online context that would support and extend their skill development and understanding? As a result, the team began to envision a whole new set of possibilities for active learning.

The team proceeded to define an educational plan: a sequence of lessons and assignments that required students to write a series of essays in which they had to provide documentation in the form of video excerpts from the digital library. This set of imagined student activities required the construction of a series of online tools, which, integrated with the digital library, permitted students to edit and annotate the selected video (see Figure 4.1). After having selected a video from the digital library, it appears in an editing and annotation area where the student can create an edit along with an annotation. Furthermore, it was projected that the excerpted video and attached notes could then be compiled as a separate individual archive in which students would be able to compose essays, annotate those essays with selected video and send completed work to both the faculty and classmates (see Figure 4.2). Edits and annotations are compiled on the left so that, when each student goes to a Workspace, they can access all their research in the digital film library and proceed to develop their essays, for which they can use their excerpted video as multimedia annotations. In this way the completed essays then become part of the discussion both online and in class.

Figure 4.1 VITAL's Video Viewer

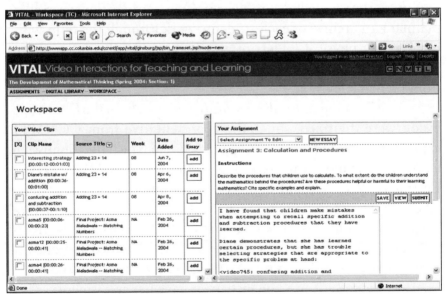

Figure 4.2 VITAL Workspace

The results of the project were that students were able to practise their skills of analysis within the data selected from the digital library of clinical interviews. Evaluations of the first two semesters' of use indicated that students had achieved a deeper understanding and higher level of skill in the domain of early childhood mathematics pedagogy and Professor Ginsburg was able to monitor and more effectively respond to student work throughout the term. VITAL has become a form of best practice at Columbia that has been taken up by others in the applied professions – social work, medicine, clinical psychiatry – and has been awarded US$2.6 million to extend its capabilities and reach a larger national audience.

Vignette 2: Assisting a French instructor, teaching intermediate French, in using the features of the discussion board of a course management system to enhance and extend meaningful conversations with her students

The instructor approached the CCNMTL wondering whether technology might provide a better way for her to give students meaningful and more timely feedback to their written compositions as well as maintain an archive of each students work through the term without keeping physical folders of papers. She was also interested in making more readily accessible video and music she had collected from French television.

As the videos and music the instructor collected from the French television were digitized, she and a representative from CCNMTL explored the possibility of creating portfolios in which the submission, feedback resubmission and process of writing essays could be supported electronically. This would allow her to communicate comments more efficiently as well as maintain a record of student progress as a natural by-product. The result was a customized discussion board of Columbia's course management system (CMS) that used its group feature to make it serve as a private conference area for each student.

After a semester's use, the instructor gave her assessment:

> I am very happy with how everything turned out and my students have let me know they like the site. You spent so much time on it and your ideas about grading compositions electronically has been a true eye-opener for me. I feel like I can grade with more care, organization and can track more easily individ-

ual grammar concerns. I see progress in each student's work each time and I know the electronic grading [including critiques and exchanges] has played a major role in that . . . The site is an integral part of the course.

These two vignettes are intended to represent two interventions that are similar in character but differ greatly in scale. In the case of the VITAL project, it represents a major investment in both curricular and software development. In the case of Intermediate French, the intervention represents a relatively modest modification of the Columbia University course management system Courseworks. What they share are certain common attributes as learning environments and the fact that they are a result of a single process.

First, the *common attributes*:

1 Both examples involve curricular and technological change with the result that each instructor can provide learning opportunities unavailable before.
2 Although each development is highly specific and was developed in response to a particular faculty member, each is also an approach applicable to a range of other courses. VITAL, as a generic technology, can enhance learning opportunities in any field where careful analysis of filmic resources supported by multimedia authoring capacity can be used to extend learning opportunities; for instance cultural theory, history of film, medicine, dentistry, social work, business or law, effectively any discipline that deals with person to person communication or the analysis of film as a medium for the conveyance of meaning. The technique deployed by the French instructor can and has been used in multiple other contexts.
3 Each project is built on the enthusiasm and initial intuition of the faculty member. At the same time, each resulting project represented a genuine collaboration in which both those who represented the Center as well as the client were able to collaborate in creating something neither party without each other had conceived at the outset.

Second, the *common process*:

- Step 1 – *Understanding the curriculum and defining the challenge.* Each project required that the faculty client and the Center representative(s) share a common understanding of the curriculum and its objectives. Just as many a homeowner chooses to buy tools before they have identified a need to use them, educational technologists are sometimes guilty of adopting technologies, as technologies, and then looking for a place to apply them. Whether one is designing a simple course site or beginning to evolve the design of a larger solution, it is important to locate all early discussions in the curricular context and its problems. With that understanding as a basis, it was then possible to identify the problematic, the challenge – that which, if not representing a deficiency, at least represents an area where significant improvement is possible.
- Step 2 – With the problem in mind, the next step in each case is to *hypothesize solutions* that include both inflections of the curricular context as well as changes in or developments of the technology.
- Step 3 – This step involves the actual *design and construction of the environment* both curricular and technological, as outlined in Step 2.
- Step 4 – *Implementation of the project in class.* In each case the delivery of the project to the faculty member by the development team does not end the service involvement. Rather, the deployment and use of the project with students should be observed and supported as much as is feasible by the educational technologist.
- Step 5 – Based on criteria developed in Step 3, the intervention must be *assessed* with the results used to either redevelop the project to increase its effectiveness or to corroborate the approach as an example of a best practice.

This cycle (understanding the curricular context and identifying the challenges, hypothesis, design, implementation and assessment) is represented by the graphic shown in Figure 4.3.

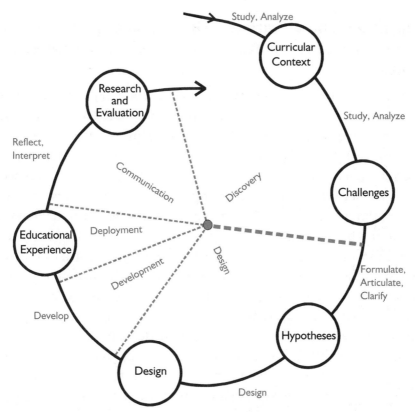

Figure 4.3 The design research process. For an animated version go to http://ccnmtl.columbia.edu/dr/page_methodology.html.

This process, which we call design research, derived from the work of Ann Brown, Allan Collins and Daniel Edelson, among others (Brown, 1992; Collins 1999; Edelson, 2002). It is the common method shared by staff and, as such, functions as a kind of cognitive software. Of course, no one person is expected to follow this in the exact order in which it is presented. Yet, any retrospective presentation of an actual engagement with a client should be able to be represented more or less by this process. The goal is that it acts as an anchor in a world of extreme motility that enables one, regardless of the different disciplines involved, to return to a common set of questions that one must answer. (See http://ccnmtl.columbia.edu/dr/index.html for further information.)

Outreach and communications: building the culture of engagement (strategies for building the campus culture)

Service sometimes implies setting up a certain capacity to respond to requests made to satisfy what can be anticipated as a routine and frequently repetitive set of needs. This is often based on a model that assumes established patterns and procedures in some dimension of institutional life that, by virtue of their character, generate certain needs so that a service enterprise is set up to address them. It is only necessary that people know that the service exists, where and what they are and when they are available. So, for example, universities have bookstores and are reasonably assured of a certain form of business based on the fact that the book is an established educational resource. The course syllabus directs students to the bookstore where they find the required texts. Reference librarians, typing pools and departmental secretaries all lived with the same level of predictability.

With the advent of digital media, however, even with the technologies we perceive as having taken root at a fundamental level for most of higher education, we are still in the early stages of building awareness of their potential as well as designing the contexts in which they become effective educational tools. For example, asynchronous bulletin boards are a common feature of CMSs but their actual use depends on how they are contextualized which, in turn, depends on the pedagogical imagination of the instructor. For many, the first hurdle to overcome is the notion that bulletin boards work on their own. Accordingly, when they are not used by students, they can't be proclaimed ineffective, as if they had independent agency. Service entities engaged in proactive efforts to recruit faculty partners must always do so in the spirit of wanting to start a conversation, specifically, pedagogical in character. This is true both for faculty using technology for the first time and those who approach with advanced interest and experience. What follows are the methods, based on experience, one might use to attract and engage faculty and administrative partners in advancing pedagogical discourse and practice related to digital technologies.

Personal contact

In a not too distant past, personal contact would have meant almost exclusively a face-to-face meeting. Now as we consider how to attract individuals to help them cross the university version of the digital divide, it is necessary to expand the concept of personal contact to include telephone calls and e-mails. A successful phone call is one that results in either a meeting or participation in a sponsored event. It is often useful to have in mind where you might direct your client on your organization website to make a specific point. Be cautious that where you direct them is accessible and does not require advanced navigation skills. In a similar manner, outreach by e-mail should provide links to sites that resonate with the interest of the potential client. All e-mails should end with invitations to something, whether it is workshop, individual meeting or presentation.

Organizational website: models of success and a manual of practice

One of the main foils any digital service enterprise has is its website. It is effectively one of the main items of the outreach toolkit. It should be conceived in the context of its potential use. In addition to providing basic information about an organization, it should provide the recruiter with demonstrations of practice as well as quick summary views of already executed projects. Faculty should be able to go to the site and see individuals like themselves providing testimony to the accessibility and effectiveness of the enterprise (www.theconference). Publications as well as grants secured should be available online. In addition, examples of project documentation, design research as well as evaluation reports should be visible to give the prospective partner a sense of the work process and its artefacts.

The site should also contain what is effectively an encyclopedia of best practice that a faculty member who is a self-starter can use to address simple needs, and educational technologists can use as a reference in discussion with faculty about a specific service. Such a resource can ultimately be useful to the organization as part of the orientation of new staff. The site should grow as practice and projects grow and be thought of as a mirror of the university's new emerging pedagogical culture driven by digital media.

Workshops, departmental presentations, faculty leading presentations, and so on

These fall into two categories, those which require that you enter the milieu of the faculty (department, full faculty or institute meetings) and others that involve inviting the faculty into your precincts, workshops, forums and seminars. There is one element shared by both that is of strategic importance. Whether you visit them or they visit you, what you present should be based on your understanding of what it is they do and how what you do can help them advance their efforts.

Realpolitik: strategic alliances within administrative hierarchies

It is no secret that every administrator with significant responsibilities has a plan of change and development on which their success hinges. It is also highly unlikely that during this time when digital technologies inspire both hope and fear they will not be part of any serious plan for the future. The greater possibility is that most university administrators so situated would welcome the opportunity to have an accomplished new media and instructional technology partner to elaborate and realize the vision.

Importance of the local media: print and electronic

University newspapers and the range of print publications (alumni, school-based or public relations fundraising instruments) as well as the websites from universities, institutions and departments have an importance in the mind of those who read them, that is greatly disproportionate to the size of their viewer or reader audience. One reads the *Times* to learn about international news and one reads the *Daily*

Falcon and looks at the .edu website to get a sense of what is happening in the university. It is important to be actively engaged in having your organization represented properly as an allure to new partners (see http://ccnmtl.columbia.edu/web/p03_press.html).

National media, conferences and publications in professional journals

Whether print or online, it is important to be a part of the professional culture that has developed around the practice of instructional technology. The professional is too young to have established habits and means for determining pedigree. Accordingly the world in which there is public discourse is uneven and sometimes discouraging but it is important, nonetheless, after exercising some discretion about it, to be part of the shaping process and have a seat at the table. This has the value of giving comfort to faculty partners that you are among the leaders in your field. For examples see: www.educause.edu/asp/ conf/ function.asp?PRODUCT_CODE=E03%2FSESS104& MEETING=e031/.

Sponsoring campus-based events

Most universities sponsor a range of non-matriculated activities open to everyone including lectures of visitors and resident scholars, panel discussions, conferences and so on. These vehicles present opportunities to reach a broad local audience. Some examples from Columbia are a biennial conference in which faculty present over the course of a day the projects completed with CCNMTL with kiosk demos available (http://ccnmtl.columbia.edu/web/p03_press. html#20031007/), the University Seminar presented four times a year to feature practitioners and theorists in the field and Center projects (http://ccnmtl.columbia.edu/nmedia/seminar/).

Securing senior faculty as partners

Perhaps one of the truly counterintuitive discoveries was that the senior faculty with tenure had the most interest and the most time to invest in new media pedagogical development, rather than the junior faculty, as some had predicted. It made sense in retrospect when one considers that the criteria for tenure, the holy grail of the untenured, still rests solidly on the quantity and character of written publications. The message is, therefore, that you identify the university's leading scholars and design your outreach strategy with them as one of its priority outreach targets. A video gives a sense of the Columbia experience. We found in the first two years more than half our clients coming from the senior ranks; see http://ccnmtl.columbia.edu/draft/video/outreach/ccnmtl_outreach_trailer.mov/.

Grants and grant getting capacity as attractors

Time and money are the commodities that all academics struggle with. Presenting one's organization as one capable of mobilizing grant efforts and having success in securing them is a natural allure for partners. It is often the case that in addition to those calls for proposals that address the field of new media and instructional technology directly, there are others aimed at research in a discipline but requiring an educational partner as a part of the dissemination plan for the research and its educational benefits. CCNMTL has received over 20 grants involving at least twice that number of faculty. See http://ccnmtl.columbia.edu/web/p03_announcements.html#20040601/ for an example of the former and http://ccnmtl.columbia.edu/projects/climate/ for an example of the latter.

Look for when the tools of research and pedagogy overlap

In this day, whether a person is learning to operate a military tank, practise performing a robotic surgical procedure, fly an airplane or develop research skills in GIS environments, it is clear that the world of education and preparation and the world of actual performance have converged. The interface and tools for the soldier, the surgeon, the pilot and the researcher are the same whether learning in simulation or engaged in the actual transactions in battle, the operating theatre, the sky or the laboratory. Only the stakes are different. The human computer interface (HCI) is 'virtually' indistinguishable in either practice mode or actual world engagement. In seeking partners one should keep in mind that faculty who have already learned to work with digital tools that are part of the practice of their 'trade' make for extraordinary partners for developing digital learning possibilities that only require contextualization (curriculum) to be effective learning environments. An example is the heart simulator developed for research, which was repurposed to become a critical component of the first year curriculum of the College of Physicians and Surgeons of Columbia University. See http://ccnmtl.columbia.edu/web/portfolio/approach_simulations_page1.html.

Service organizations as growing networks: building intramural strategic relationships

We are at the beginning of discovering the institutional arrangements suitable to the evolution of the purposeful use of technology in education. This means that we are trying to do new things either in old structures or new structures that have emerged in silo manner to answer discrete needs. The interest of any entity seeking to provide service and encourage the creative pedagogical use of digital media and technology is to make alliances with like and overlapping organizations. Conversations of this kind begin by establishing a common purpose and then discovering the practical areas of overlap whereby both entities might accomplish more together than apart. Here are some recommendations for building intra-university strategic relationships:

1 Look for *partnerships with existing organizations* that have specialized functions, such as departmental homegrown technical groups or content-specific cross-departmental groups. Seek to

create alliances with them with the argument and intention that a combination of their resources and yours can multiply each of your capacities to be effective in your field. An example of such partnerships at Columbia University is the five-year-old collaboration between CCNMTL and the Learning Resources Group of the School of Social Work, which has led to innovation and significant incorporation of IT in the teaching and learning practice of the faculty. See http://ccnmtl.columbia.edu/web/news_archives/cat_2001.shtml.

2 *Reorganize to create satellites and office extensions* so that services and development can be in greater physical proximity to the target faculty. Despite the litany of praise for the unimportance of physical location in the digital age, the chant of ubiquity of access to a ubiquity of resources, the fact is that physical proximity matters a lot, especially to those who have not experimented with digital communication environments, often our target client. An example of this tactic at Columbia University is the development of the Medical Center offices of CCNMTL, which has been the locus of significant pedagogical innovation in medicine, dentistry, nursing and public health.

3 *Build strong relationships with digital organizations which have compatible functions* related to the technical platform as well as information provision. At Columbia University, since 2003 CCNMTL has been part of a single organization called Information Services, which includes libraries, electronic publishing and academic information systems, and is responsible for maintaining generic academic applications such as e-mail and a database solution. Before that organizational structure was created, the CCNMTL had partnered ACIS (Columbia's Academic Information Systems department) in the construction of Columbia's CMS entitled 'Courseworks', and the libraries on a number of projects such as the Virtual Tapes Collection, which supports the required core Music and Humanities course of Columbia College.

4 *Build bridges through the sharing of personnel* who can effect and give life to the commitments organizations make to advance each other's common purposes. At Columbia University the Director of Digital Arts at the School of the Arts also works for CCNMTL and has effectively provided ongoing and effective outreach to the School of Arts faculty. A similar relationship is being constructed through the creation of a new staff member who will bridge CCNMTL and the Language Resource Center with a mission to advance purposeful language pedagogy.

A mini-handbook for the practitioner

So much of what a service organization can accomplish occurs in the clinches between the educational technologist, the front line operative and the faculty client. An educational technologist must remember that neither technology nor pedagogy alone is the issue and that one must be an educationally savvy technologist and a technology savvy educator. What follows is a guide for those who are on the line.

1 *Listen before you leap: understand the client's goals before suggesting an approach.* Do not immediately recommend a solution based on a 'similar' situation until all the facts are in. Remember that the intelligence and utility of anything you do for a client will proceed from your understanding of the client's approach as well as the content of the discipline.
2 *Honestly represent the learning curve of mastering a technology as a mediating environment that comes between a teacher and the students.* A delicate balance. The technologist should honestly state the investment expected of the client, but be clear that proper supports would be put in place. If clients invest nothing in a project, they will not use it (http://ccnmtl.columbia.edu/web/news_ archives/cat_2001.shtml).
3 *Be sensitive to the degree a client is invested in the project.* It is often the case that the success of the simplest intervention will depend on whether the client is invested. Accordingly you not only

have to listen to understand clients' goals but also on another level to discern the degree of conviction they have to see things through. Even if you judge that conviction is low, you will still be better able to build supports intended to raise the level of confidence.

4   *Do not get lost in headlights of the technology.* Be sure to remember that ultimately student learning is the goal. You should know and continue to learn a broad range of pedagogical tactics and curricular approaches. The technologist should be well versed in theory and classroom practice. The nimbleness of your response will be in part dependent on your level of ease and comfort as an educational thinker.

5   *Understand the value added of a broad range of technologies.* For example, you should critically examine when and how to recommend digital audio and video over traditional tapes, digital images over slides, e-text over coursepacks, and so on. You must understand the utility and purpose of technologies well enough to present cogently the potential value added for study and learning. In addition, staying abreast of new emergent applications and tools is essential.

6   *Stay sensitive to the degree to which you live embedded in the jargon of our field and how important it is to not alienate people with technobabble.* You should explain complex technical concepts clearly and succinctly, and in the simplest way you know. Technical mumbo-jumbo does not impress or inform clients, it distances them. Remember that most clients are interested in the effects, not the means.

7   *Begin simple with new clients: an initial small success in the long run will be more important to the longevity of your working relationship than a spectacular near miss.* Getting people interested in new things is a gentle art that is best practised with the open hand rather than the rhetorical bear trap. Try to keep in mind how you feel when you are with an expert in a field in which you know little and how quickly one is tempted to abandon ship and seek the shores of what you know.

8 *Never over-design the interface; stay focused on the learning calculus of what you are making.* Do not yield to the seductiveness of the visual universe. Understand exactly what you are trying to facilitate in respect to what people will be able to think and do as a result of your effort with a client. This does not necessarily include eliciting the responses 'nice' and 'cool'. Interesting design is important, but fancy aesthetics will not compensate for an inadequate pedagogical and functional design.

9 *Support does not end with a completed website: be attentive to your clients after they have left.* Remember that the client, no matter how skilled and adept at other things, is often at the beginning with digital media. With often no repertoire of learned behaviors to fall back on, simple obstacles can be experienced as monumental. Helping your client through those moments of distress can determine success or failure.

10 *Create an environment where a technological failure does not lead to a pedagogical failure.* Technology should supplement, extend and potentially transform teaching, not make teaching subservient to it. All beginning efforts with new clients should focus on the development of hybrid or blended environments in which experiences not technologically dependent complement those facilitated by the technology. Think of it as a person learning to swim in a pool, always a side to grab, rather than in the middle of the ocean.

11 *Build in order to learn.* Remember that what you are creating are visible heuristics, 'objects' in the popular lingo, which serve the two purposes of supporting faculty teaching and student learning as well as acting as vehicles of discovery. You are the creators of a field more than being adepts in an established field. There is much to learn from what has been done but the possibilities for innovation eclipse the accomplishments of the past.

12 *Learn how to shift perspectives.* Seek to build habits based on success and out of those habits and successes come best practices. At the same time slavish habits and the traps of language can stymie the imagination necessary for invention. Stay nimble and devise

methods for dislocating yourself from your embeddedness. These methods range from reading things that overlap your interests but would be *liber non gratus* in the field (for example, Neil Stephenson's *Snow Crash*) to attending conferences not only in the field but also orthogonal to the field. Metaphorically, the challenge is to go places where you are not supposed to be or expected to go.[4]

13 *Keep the design research spiral active in your mind.* Even in discussions with faculty ostensibly simple in character, keep in mind the spiral of design research. Keep it running 'in the back' like a piece of software that can provide you with the bases you might touch however lightly as you proceed. Simply: curriculum context, problematic, hypothesis, design and construction, evaluation.

14 *Never say, 'No, we don't do that.'* This does not mean that you do everything. Rather, it means that as a service enterprise you either directly provide the service or help the person find the service they need. For example, CCNMTL does not build organizational websites but when the Pulitzer Prize people approached us for help with their site, we consulted them and after three meetings helped to connect them to the right group to solve their problem.

Final word: living in interesting times

We live at a fecund moment in the history of communications, technology and education. In fact there were only two other times remotely like it in western history: the 5th century in Athens dazzled and confused by the advent of the alphabet and Early Modernity struggling with the forces unleashed by printing. In both instances the world of education, knowledge production and storage, and communications changed in ways hard to predict from the vantage point of those enmeshed. Looking back we are tempted to see the results as determined, the only possible direction things might have gone. Yet as Ronald J. Deibert points out (1997, 17–44), human choice and other converging influences contributed to the ecology of causation that produced the world we know. Determinism is the illusion of hind-sight.

Human agency, imagination and intellect have their greatest moments in fertile chaotic times, times when vision and invention matter, and conformity and slavish habit have no rewards. Those of us who are in the trenches of organizations seeking to reinvent the enterprise of education must shoulder the task of carrying the past but with an eye to the new world that awaits our efforts in order for it to be. We must strive to see ourselves as servants in the interest of the invention of e-learning, simultaneously seeking to build habits of good practice but remaining aware that all habit eventually obscures our vision and our capacity to see beyond our immediate horizons. We are the architects of the imagined worlds within which people learn and study. We have just begun to glimpse the possibil-ities.

Notes

1   Black, J. D. and McClintock, R. O. (1995) An Interpretation Construction Approach to Constructivist Design, in Wilson, B. (ed.), *Constructivist Learning Environment*, Englewood Cliffs, NJ, Educational Technology Publications; Nix, D. (1988) Should Computers Know What You Can Do With Them?, *Teachers College Record*, **89** (3); Harel, I. and Papert, S. (1991) *Constructionism*, Norwood, NJ, Ablex Publishing Corporation.

2   See National Science Foundation Report: Knowledge Lost in Information: report of the NSF Workshop on Research Directions for Digital Libraries, June 15–17, Chatham, MA, specifically, 3.3.2, 17–18, Cognition Leveraging Tools, where following Jonassen, D. H. and Reeves, T. C., Learning with Technology: Using Computers as Cognitive Tools, in *Handbook of Research for Educational Communications and Technology*, New York, Macmillan Library Reference USA, 1996, 693–719, there is the recognition that tools within digital

libraries . . . will help insure that the nations cyber-infrastructure is an active, not a passive place, for learning.

3 Carol Twigg in an interview published in *Educause Review*: Teaching and Learning in a Hybrid World: an interview with Carol Twigg, July/August 2004, 53, comments: 'I understand learning objects as pieces of learning materials that can be mixed and matched to create a learning experience for students. A learning object could be a simulation in chemistry or an exercise in mathematics or an assessment in fine arts. The notion is that you can take pieces at different levels of granularity and put them together to create a learning experience. Tutorial programs certainly are part of that mix.' Twigg is struggling to describe learning objects and make some room for interactivity and the world of the learner but seems to still focus on objects as if they educate autonomously.

4 At the same time as we must work to shift perspectives, there is no question – as Shirley Ann Jackson alerts us in *Educause Review*, Ahead of the Curve: future shifts in high education, January/February 2004, **18** – that the evolution of technology itself provides disruption, potentially creative, if one seizes the opportunity for deep discussion. In her own words: 'What we know now is that we must be prepared for disruption. Technology is disruptive. Information technology is really disruptive. Colleges and universities must engage in broad-based, grassroots, deep discussions, must think through the issues and their impact on higher education.'

References

Black, J. D. and McClintock, R. O. (1995) An Interpretation Construction Approach to Constructivist Design. In Wilson, B. (ed.), *Constructivist Learning Environment*, Englewood Cliffs, NJ, Educational Technology Publications.

Brown, A. L. (1992) Design Experiments: theoretical and methodological challenges in creating complex interventions in classroom settings, *Journal of the Learning Sciences*.

Collins, A. (1999) The Changing Infrastructure of Education Research. In Lagemann, E. C. and Shulman, L. S. (eds), *Education Research: problems and possibilities*, San Francisco, Jossey-Bass.

Deibert, R. J. (1997) *Parchment, Printing, and Hypermedia: communication in world order transformation*, New York, Columbia University Press.

Edelson, D. (2002) Design Research: what we learn when we engage in design, *Journal of the Learning Sciences*.

Harel, I. and Papert, S. (1991) *Constructionism*, Norwood, NJ, Ablex Publishing Corporation.

Jackson, S. A. (2004) Ahead of the Curve: future shifts in high education, *Educause Review*, (January/February).

Jonassen, D. H. and Reeves, T. C. (1996) Learning with Technology: using computers as cognitive tools. In *Handbook of Research for Educational Communications and Technology*, New York, Macmillan Library Reference USA.

McLean, N. and Lynch, C. (2004) Interoperability Between Library Information Services and Learning Environments – Bridging the Gaps, A Joint White Paper on Behalf of the IMS Global Learning Consortium and the Coalition for Networked Information, 10 May.

Nix, D. (1988) Should Computers Know What You Can Do With Them?, *Teachers College Record*, **89** (3).

Stephenson, N. (1992) *Snow Crash*, New York, Doubleday.

Twigg, C. (2004) Teaching and Learning in a Hybrid World: an interview with Carol Twigg, *Educause Review*, July/August.

5

Just one piece of the jigsaw: e-literacy in the wider perspective

Peter Stubley

Introduction

In spite of the best intentions of librarians and the substantial efforts that go into the process, elements from the literature of user education, information skills and information literacy keep floating to the surface to remind me of one of the quotations at the beginning of Len Deighton's *Horse Under Water*:

> Perhaps the worst plight of a vessel is to be caught in a gale on a lee-shore. In this connection the following . . . rules should be observed:
>   1. Never allow your vessel to be found in such a predicament . . .

One would hope that the plights would have changed, or the gales blown out, but a recent book on the topic (Martin and Rader, 2003) suggests that forces preventing us from delivering truly effective user education may not be so much different in the 21st century than they were 30 years ago. Unappreciative and ignorant teaching staff, lack of institutional commitment, unreceptive and reluctant students are sometimes viewed with the wide-eyed disbelief of a missionary in 19th-century Africa. The message is so wonderful, painless and life-supporting, why isn't my hand being bitten off?

Even though the earlier user education has evolved through information skills to information literacy and its detailed definition – in the UK – through SCONUL's 'Seven Pillars' model (Corrall and Hathaway, 2000; Johnson, 2003), it remains largely a rarefied confection, a tool developed by librarians for librarians and little appreciated outside the profession. The Seven Pillars model itself represents a wide-ranging and serious attempt to move the debate on information skills forward, raising its profile in higher education in particular, though it is still too early to say what the overall impact across institutions will be. But while blame continues to be directed towards 'the academic' – and Godwin (2003), McGuinness (2003) and Town (2003) all report instances of this – I would suggest that the situation will never improve, even with support from the most refined structures in the world. However many pillars we use, librarians will never escape their self-obsessed predicament and be able to sail free from the lee shore.

Sailing free will only be achieved once the waters have been mapped, the weather report considered – however variable and unpredictable – and the crew and boat checked for sea-worthiness. The action can be pursued in isolation, irrespective of all these influences, but the chances of success will be much greater if all prevailing forces are taken into consideration. The essence of this chapter is that information literacy is no different and that to achieve maximum impact it must be pursued in the widest possible context within the institution: it is not the whole, it is but one piece of the jigsaw created from the interface between the library and the environment in which it operates. Implementing library strategy for the maximum benefit of an institution means that on some occasions the focus of services will fall on information literacy, while on others the emphasis may be elsewhere but, if the services are developed synergistically, they can be delivered in ways most appropriate for different situations.

It is not only library services that form the necessary wider context in which information literacy should be considered but the environment in which they operate: technical and pedagogic approaches to the delivery of learning, teaching and skills taken by the institution; perceptions and shortcomings of library services in the eyes of academic staff and students; and the expectations, abilities, study patterns and work–life balance of students in relation not only to the course being taken but to the institution as a whole and national policies that impact on all of these, directly or indirectly.

Apart from the wider contextualization, the other leitmotif running through this chapter is embedding. To be truly effective, an information skills resource needs to be embedded in at least four ways:

- in the course which the student is undertaking to gain a qualification
- within the library services being delivered to the student to support his or her learning and teaching
- with the wider full range of study skills considered by the institution or the individual department as key to the full understanding of the course or programme
- within the technical infrastructure – such as a virtual learning environment (VLE) – that forms the delivery mechanism for the learning and teaching. Through an extension of the use of the word, one might add a fifth way: embedding into the 'acceptance system' of students, getting them to appreciate that information skills are useful and are worth spending time on mastering.

By interweaving these themes, providing wider background contexts through links to the education literature and commenting on some current information literacy practice, the chapter explains how recent work at the University of Sheffield Library is attempting to forge a new partnership with academic colleagues and thereby provide improved learning and teaching support services to students that incorporate information skills provision.

A word about terminology

There is no shortage of contributions to be found in the debate on information skills, information literacy, information fluency or, more recently and stressing the electronic, e-literacy. Any recent publication will include comparisons and recommendations and Martin and

Rader (2003), a collection of 25 essays, is a good place to start. Indeed, in that book, Johnson (2003), in outlining the work of the SCONUL Task Force that developed the Seven Pillars approach, says 'we have continued to use the term "information skills" for what we are interested in, rather than formulations such as information literacy or information handling'. It is recognized that 'information literacy' broadly assumes the practice of higher-level skills and a wider understanding than simply 'doing' but, for the purposes of this chapter the terms have been used interchangeably.

Similarly, Martin's (2003) description of e-literacy makes it unnecessary to attempt to redefine it here:

> by e-literacy I mean the awarenesses, skills, understandings and reflective-evaluative approaches that are necessary for an individual to operate comfortably in information-rich and IT-supported environments. An individual is e-literate to the extent that they have acquired these awarenesses, skills and approaches.

This chapter deliberately focuses on the key issues surrounding information skills, information literacy and e-literacy rather than the components that make up each and which might form part of taught courses.

The student in the 21st century

The nature of the student body

Even without engaging in a discussion of the rosy good old days, many signals suggest that students entering higher education today bring with them to university different abilities, expectations and values when compared with their forebears. In 1997, the report on the National Committee of Inquiry into Higher Education (NCIHE) – the Dearing Report – was published and, in the introductory discussion on the nature of the student body (NCIHE, 1997, 17–28) it recognized that the character of the student body had changed with the dramatic increase in the number of people entering higher education. All teaching staff who had been working at their present institution for at least five years were asked whether, over that period, they felt that the quality of students had changed, and approximately half said that in the case of undergraduates this had declined. The Report emphasized that it was not clear whether these concerns related to the wider range of qualifications achieved by students or a perceived decline of those with conventional qualifications, or both. Those teaching undergraduates were also asked to specify the frequency with which they felt they had to compensate for subject knowledge and competencies (communication skills, numeracy skills, and so on) that should have been covered before entry into higher education and one in four said this was necessary for subject knowledge, one in three for competencies.

Informal discussion with academic colleagues suggests that the NCIHE survey did not identify an isolated instance of the lack of preparedness among new higher education students and the education literature suggests this is not confined to the UK. Boyd et al. (1998) reported from Australia 'that there is a commonly held opinion amongst university teaching staff that students, especially at first year, do not have the requisite numeracy and literacy skills required to perform adequately within tertiary education' and discussed methods of encouraging students to improve performance. File (1984) indicates that this is not an entirely new problem, reporting that first year students at the University of Cape Town had difficulties arising from lecturers who assumed greater knowledge on the part of students than they actually possessed and that too much reading was prescribed, making it difficult to keep up.

A number of recent studies have taken these concerns as their starting point, discussed them from a social and political perspective and explored the issues in more detail through interviews with students. While only occasionally raising issues about libraries and information skills, these papers can provide additional insights on the implementation of e-literacy programmes. Winn (2002) begins by describing Kneale's 'strategic student' (1997) who 'devotes more time to social activities and employment than to study and appears to have little or no interest in the degree subject', exhibiting 'poor attendance at classes which did not contribute directly to assessment'. She deftly outlines the factors that have led to the massification, commodification and vocationalism of UK higher education and the rise in the number of non-traditional students through widening participation measures.

In investigating student motivation, the interviewees were broadly categorized into three groups – students with demands but who could nevertheless undertake the amount of study expected for a full-time degree course; students with responsibilities that gave them little time for academic work; and students who had few commitments but spent little time studying – though it was recognized that a fourth group does exist – students with few commitments who devote substantial time to academic work – but was not represented in this survey. It is clear that the strategic student still exists and one member of the 'few commitments/minimal study' group expressed the oft-presumed but rarely uttered statement that, 'We sit in the bar in between lectures. We should be in the library, but the appeal of the bar is too great.' Winn concludes that 'evidence of rapidly declining motivation, and difficulties in fulfilling good intentions about study habits, suggests that harnessing students' early enthusiasm for academic work and assisting them to develop the skills necessary for independent learning' might be a way forward.

Students' skills needs

In taking a wider view of the topic of e-literacy, it is instructive to delve into the education literature and to see that, in spite of the extensive coverage of 'skills', information skills and information literacy rarely appear explicitly on the agenda. Which is not to say that they are ignored concepts – they are not, as what follows will show – rather that their discussion is considered as part of wholescale skills requirements of students. This is also, to an extent, reflected in the number of generic skills-based 'how to study' handbooks available (see, for example, Cottrell, 1999; Northedge, 1990; Race, 1999; Rowntree, 1998).

Lizzio and Wilson (2004) point out that different stakeholder groups such as students, academics and employers perceive skills in quite different ways (which brings to mind the perhaps not apocryphal story of the company executive who, when asked what he understood by communication skills said, 'They do what I tell them'). The authors went on to produce a list of skills that were potentially relevant to the learning, living and working aspects of a student's life, arriving at 14 skills domains. Nine of these domains were generic capabilities – self-management; interpersonal; adaptability and learning; problem-solving and decision-making; conceptual and analytical; team and group; oral communication; written communication; and information management; and five describe capabilities specific to areas of application – career and vocational management; organizational membership; community and citizenship; personal effectiveness; and professional effectiveness. The design of programmes of study at institutional, faculty and departmental levels must balance the teaching of core with subsidiary subjects and incorporate those skills domains considered to be a good fit with the discipline, all in a way that appeals to potential students to apply and register for courses. In these circumstances it is difficult to make a case for special consideration to be given to information literacy but, equally, it becomes frustrating when it is ignored.

In addition to providing the 'skills schema' described above, Lizzio and Wilson applied it to first year students (at an Australian university) to gain an insight into their perceptions of skills: how did they value them and what did they value? By sub-dividing the 14 skills domains, a total of 168 items was created which the students had to rate by perceived importance and relevance. The categorization of skills so produced indicated six primary factors – professional skills; writing and literacy skills; problem-solving; communication and leadership; conceptual thinking; and membership and responsibility – several of which combined items from the original domains into this new structure. It is particularly interesting that what had been structured as two separate domains in the original schema – written communication and information management – were seen by the students as closely linked. However, students rated all skill areas – except written communication and information management – as more relevant to their future work than their present course of study. The three disciplines tested were behavioural science, engineering and management and the authors say that the testing of students from the arts and humanities should be a matter for future investigation.

Sutherland (2003) concentrated on the perceptions and use of study skills by first year (nursing) students in Scotland. The investigation arose from similar concerns to those expressed by Winn (2002) about the effects of widening participation and the need for greater levels of support for first years: 'Instead of higher education being the prerogative of the "above average" pupils, more of the pupils classified as "average" at school are also now starting higher education.' The study was undertaken to assess how this group was coping with the demands of university, in addition to considering the reactions of mature students entering without conventional qualifications. While the sample was small (three first year students on a foundation course and seven second years), the interview technique enabled detailed responses to be obtained and showed 'huge differences between the unsophisticated young learners straight from school and the unsophisticated mature learners (on the one hand) and the sophisticated mature learners (on the other hand)'. Some students exhibited a surface approach to the understanding and use of study skills, others a deep approach, though essay writing was identified as the most demanding task by both surface and deep learners. Sutherland found that most of his sample were 'strategic' pupils at school, doing just enough to pass, and he concludes that 'there seems to be a need to improve the provision of study skill courses in both high schools and institutes of higher education and – most important of all – in the transition between them'.

Academic staff and skills

The relationship between library staff and academics, particularly in the area of information skills training, has been the subject of much debate over 30 years. The balanced, co-operative approach proffered by Farber (1999), though qualified over the years and moulded to changing circumstances, can stand in stark contrast to almost militant statements about blame and the need to take responsibility into the librarian's own hands. An example of this is a debate reported by Powis (2000) where 'several speakers pointed out that many academics are not interested in teaching anything . . . and are consequently often very bad teachers of their subjects . . . they often do not have any information skills themselves and have little idea how to teach them . . . their focus is very narrow'. The lack of any wider perspective is particularly disappointing given that this conference was held so recently (it was not held in the 'early days' of user education) and that the debate followed on from what, I would argue, was clearly too provocative a presentation from Heseltine (2000), who argued that the only way that students would engage with such skills was if they were 'firmly embedded in a subject context'.

Rarely is this state of affairs seen in relation to the facts of academic life, or if it is, these are rarely acknowledged outright from the library perspective. Hardesty (1999) mentions the stresses faced by academics but only in passing, virtually treating it as a normal fact of life, something inextricably linked with 'the life of the mind'. Jenkins, Breen and Lindsay (2003) outline the impact that national policies (particularly in the UK) have had at an institutional level and how they have created a situation where 'teaching and research compete for the time, energy and attention of lecturers' making it 'the disaster area of the decade'. The situation that has given rise to widespread feelings of frustration is succinctly described in the following quotation:

In the UK the national mechanisms for judging teaching (the Quality Assurance Agency), and for judging and rewarding research (the Research Assessment Exercise), have operated to deliver carrots and administer sticks, each in studied ignorance and splendid isolation from the other. Within universities an identical self-defeating strategy has been followed, usually by threatening the same academic staff with redundancy if they do not teach more students with diminishing resources and if they do not publish more papers, attract more research funding and take on more consultancy work. At the same time as they exhort academics to produce more research for the benefit of the university, institutions disregard evidence that the result is a weekly workload which breaches the European Union's Working Time Directive, by treating research and teaching as if they were private goods resulting from free individual choice.

(Jenkins, Breen and Lindsay, 2003, 50)

Published in 2003, the book cited papers from 1996 in support of this statement. Things have not improved in the intervening years and it is against this backdrop – with the added burden of departmental and course administrative duties – that discussions about information literacy programmes need to be viewed.

Tensions clearly existed with the introduction of government skills agendas supported by employers' claims for personal transferable skills in preference to subject-based technical knowledge, creating 'scepticism among university tutors to this view of university education, who believe it is not part of their role to provide skills for employment' (Bennett, Dunne and Carré, 1999). And, as indicated by McAvinia and Oliver (2002), 'the values of academic staff may not be the values of the skills initiative, and in many cases the development of transferable skills will be outside the traditions and experience of the department'. However, 'many universities have accepted the implications of the political and economic agenda, at least at the level of policy' (Bennett, Dunne and Carré, 1999) and the current education literature, just a fraction of which has been represented in this chapter, is full of discussions of the best approaches to take to skill teaching and acquisition and related issues such as student-centred learning. It should not automatically be assumed that all academic staff are reluctant to consider new ideas or are unaware of the needs for skills training but these issues have to be balanced with everything else. And, Heseltine (2000) again, in talking about the capabilities of academic staff to teach key skills, said, 'I know from experience that the best staff do this brilliantly.'

The only point on which I would take issue with Farber (1999) in his excellent description of 30 years of the academic–librarian co-operation – and he does emphasize that it 'still seems to me that the most sensible, most practical relationship is a co-operative one' – is his use of the word 'problem' to describe the relationship, a fact compounded by Shirato in the two short paragraphs of introduction to the Farber paper where it states 'success in this area has been hard-won, as his article makes clear, and in many ways the battle is not yet won'. I do not wish to come over as sounding politically correct, but use of words such as 'problem', 'hard-won' and 'battle' are not the best way of encouraging a dialogue among equals, a dialogue which might hope to investigate collaborative working for the benefit of students.

Improved dialogue?

Recent work at the University of Sheffield can be used as an example of the ways in which the relationship between library staff and academics might be improved. In 2001, the University of Sheffield Library successfully bid for a Learning and Teaching Development Grant aimed at supporting excellence and innovation in learning and teaching across the institution by underpinning developments and initiatives in the University's Learning and Teaching Strategy. The vast majority of grants had been made to pump-prime initiatives in academic departments but this Library bid was supported because of its institution-wide potential; it was called 'a collaborative model for the integration of library services into WebCT'.

The project was planned in two stages: a user needs survey to gauge student and academic staff requirements, to be followed by the building and evaluation of a prototype based on the outcomes of the survey. The results of the survey were particularly illuminating and were instrumental in causing a re-appraisal of library services in three ways: developing co-ordinated services for the University's emerging VLE; re-thinking the provision of information skills and e-literacy;

and re-invigorating more widely library services in support of learning and teaching.

The user needs survey consisted of in-depth interviews with academic staff across the whole institution about their use of WebCT for course delivery, the reactions of their students to the technology, and their particular requirements and use of information resources, irrespective of whether these were library-based or web-based. The ten academics were chosen either for their extensive and direct experience of using WebCT or, as heads of department or directors of learning and teaching development, being responsible for decision-making in this area. they were also deliberately selected from across all seven faculties of the university, to ensure that a wide range of viewpoints was gathered.

Out of the ensuing discussions, two key areas emerged: University policy and progress with WebCT; and the information requirements of courses. In terms of policy, the University of Sheffield is well advanced. Its Learning and Teaching Strategy is in place, directors of learning and teaching development have been appointed to co-ordinate activities across faculties, and departmental policies for moving forward with WebCT are emerging. As with many new technologies, initial uptake of the technology has relied to a large extent on enthusiasts though it was interesting to find that these were far from the usual 'techies', investigating the software for its own ends, but rather academics interested in improving the learning and teaching process for their students. Even though, at the time of the interviews (February and March 2002), take-up might have been described as patchy, the use of WebCT across the University was substantial, with 7500 student users on 203 modules.

In stark contrast to the Library's established methodology for handling reading lists, the incorporation of information resources within WebCT courses was found to be anything but standard and had arisen in an organic way, developing with components of modules and following the different teaching approaches of the academics concerned. Very rarely had the simple method been used of references being listed at the end of an electronic page and in several cases information resources had not even been included – in particular where the WebCT modules were considered as being supplementary to the paper-based or traditional elements of the course.

Discussions with academic staff also identified serious limitations in the library software used for handling reading lists, in particular, in its inabilities to handle annotations and to organize the lists in accordance with teaching delivery (for example by relevance of text, by week and by prioritizing readings). It became very clear that the imposition of a single, monolithic solution for handling information resources in WebCT would not provide the type of user-focused services that the library was looking for in this new environment; for that matter, neither would this prove acceptable to the academics consulted.

The relevance of reading lists and the use made of these in an electronic environment were also questioned. For example, do students find any real value in having an electronic version of their reading lists in WebCT when, in many cases, a link to the Library OPAC simply tells them about the availability of the item in the library, located at some distance from the desktop where they are currently working? As one interviewee (a registered student on a Masters course in addition to being an academic) said, 'When I'm working at 11 o'clock at night, I don't want to be told a book is in the Library where I can't get hold of it; I want it to be delivered to me electronically, straight away.' In other words, increasingly when students have course content delivered online via the VLE, they will naturally expect that the bulk of their supporting reading should be made available in precisely this same way.

The solutions that the library implemented as a result of these discussions are described later in this chapter. Suffice to say at this stage that the process itself, engaging in a two-way, open dialogue with academic staff, ultimately changed the library service. Why was this? First, many of the interviewees had not often – or at all – had an opportunity to talk about their specific problems, or be prompted to explore how the library might improve services *to them and their students*. At Sheffield much of the dialogue occurs between two individuals – the academic liaison librarian in the library and the departmental library representative, a member of academic staff in the department – and, although communication lines evolve in complex ways, some academics can remain untouched by the Library. Furthermore, the discussion focused on the academics' teaching needs and, in this wide-ranging way, touched on topics such as problem-based learning, task-based learning, the enthusiasms and Luddite tendencies of students towards the VLE, hardware and network problems, the different approaches taken by individuals, departments and faculties towards electronic course delivery, ideas of blended learning and, inevitably, a catalogue of drawbacks about current library services, sometimes where these had little bearing on WebCT course delivery.

At the outset of the project it was never anticipated that such a wide variety of topics would emerge from the interviews and it is never a comfortable experience learning of the drawbacks of one's services. But, what came out of the process, not only from the interviews but from further discussion and reflection over the following months, was a wider understanding by the Library of how the learning and teaching was changing in the University in response to student and institutional needs, and what steps the Library must take if it wanted to stay relevant in an ever-changing environment.

Information skills in an electronic environment

In addition to the lessons learnt from the dialogue with academics, it became clear that the library required a facility for managing information resources if it was to play an active role in the university's VLE. After testing the functionality of one of the reading list software packages on the market – in this case TalisList – it was seen that it could provide significant benefits by enabling links to be created to any digital object, irrespective of traditional format of that object: individual electronic journal papers; electronic journal contents pages; bibliographic databases; web pages; subject gateways; video clips, audio clips and image files; in addition to metadata from the Library OPAC which in turn could be linked to circulation details. This facility, coupled with the abilities to annotate individual entries for the benefits of students and to organize the list to mirror course delivery, caused a complete re-think on what the old-fashioned reading list might become: to such an extent that this has now been re-named a resource list.

In the two years since the completion of the Learning and Teaching Development Grant project, all old-style lists have been transferred to TalisList and many – via the New Partnership initiative described in the final section of this chapter – have been converted to resource lists. In addition, through a pilot investigation of 'electronic offprints', papers that would not be available electronically through the normal channels have been digitized and made accessible to students following the payment of the copyright fee (Freeman and Parker, 2004).

As a result of the success of the Library's first Learning and Teaching Development Grant and discussions at steering group level between academics and library staff, a second grant was later awarded to develop 'an information skills resource for WebCT'. The approaches taken by the two projects are seen as complimentary, resource lists providing stress-free access to course readings leading to encouragement of exploration in guided and more open ways, and the information skills resource a way-station in the VLE, to be visited in times of need but which also delivers skills quotas at key points throughout the course. At the time of writing (late 2004), the WebCT-based information skills resource is mid-way through its development. Some content has been written and tested with students and the resulting feedback has influenced the further design. This iterative process, together with close working with academic staff from four departments and focus groups of students, should ensure that the resource has real validity when it is made available across the University.

This quotation from McAvinia and Oliver (2002) informed both the framing of the information skills bid to the University and the subsequent construction of the resource:

If web-based support for central initiatives is likely to be effective, its design must be sensitive to the context in which it is to be used and the specific tensions attendant upon its adoption. This implies that the role of the designer needs to be different when working with such initiatives than when creating self-contained applications or resources within specific departmental cultures.

While discussions in the library and information science community have often compared subject-based and generic information skills approaches, there is little in the literature on the practical application of the latter. The Open University has developed SAFARI, a generic web-based resource (Dillon et al., 2003) but there appears to have been little else. The reason for this might be that, while the majority of information skills sessions are provided face-to-face, and to groups of students with similar subject interests, there is no significant incentive to develop generic methods. By contrast, at Sheffield, the focus of the bid was to create an electronic-only resource that would be accessible solely from within the VLE and also available right across the University, making a generic design the only practicable choice.

Currently, the Library does not have a remit to create and deliver a credit-based module for undergraduates and the University has taken the approach that skills should not be centrally co-ordinated but delivered through the programmes of each department. In this environment it was a coup to have the University approve the bid – via the Learning Development and Media Unit and the Pro-Vice Chancellor for Learning and Teaching – and it was felt that success was less to do with the content than the robust statements about collaborative working with departments to ensure that the resource was embedded into their courses to support learning objectives.

McAvinia and Oliver (2002) present four models – slightly modified from Drew, Shaw and Mowthorpe (2000) – for the way skills can be incorporated into courses from central provision:

1 *Optional model*. Materials are recommended by tutors or in course documents but the student is left to search them out and use

them at their own discretion; no formal training is provided and there is no formal relationship with specific parts of the course.

2 *Directed model*. Materials are recommended by tutors or in course documents and students get formal introduction and training in their use and are directed to them from time to time, but these are not strongly identified with specific parts of the course.

3 *Integrated model*. Materials are recommended, formal introduction is provided, students are directed to materials at appropriate points of the course and tutors associate materials with course or module delivery.

4 *Contextualized model*. Materials are recommended and training provided; students are directed to use materials at appropriate points and tutors contextualize the materials for use in their course.

Clearly one would like to work with either the integrated or context-ualized model and this is the intention – or hope – at Sheffield. Embedding the information skills resource into individual courses not only provides the context and meaning to students when they are investigating individual skills but also supplies the channel for deliv-ering subject-based support from a generic core. At the same time, as mentioned above, the whole information skills resource – not simply individual subject sections – will still be available for students to dip into and use as they need to answer wider queries not incor-porated into the embedding.

Assessment will play a crucial role in the embedding process and it is the intention to work with academics to identify the learning objectives for the use of information skills in their courses and then to develop suitable assessments, using the facilities within WebCT as appropriate. As far as possible, it is intended to follow the good prac-tice detailed by Webber and Johnston (2003): 'assessment will be varied, so that it is relevant to the particular area of information lit-eracy being learnt, and also connects with real-world applications and problems where appropriate . . . a blend of self, expert and peer assessment will encourage reflection and critical awareness, which is informed by "expert" summative and formative feedback'. Early evaluation has indicated that some students prefer to forego the information skills content and go directly to diagnostic tests to receive feedback about their level of understanding and these levels of self-assessment will be further developed as the resource grows.

To deliver the embedding required into departmental courses, the Library is focusing on the potential of the learning object because 'its use and reuse, its discovery and shareability, its existence as a dig-ital entity and the context in which it can be used are the key elements to creating broader, interinstitutional applications of technology and learning and teaching' (OCLC, 2003; for more details on learning objects, see Boyle, 2003). During 2004, the University of Sheffield is moving from the Campus Edition of WebCT to Vista, piloting with one key department over two semesters and moving fully to the new system from September 2005. From early investigations, Vista appears to offer a number of opportunities for delivering learning objects and as both the information skills content and the pilot Vista imple-mentation progresses, different ways of 'slicing' the resource into manageable learning objects that match with the learning objec-tives of courses will be explored. The plan is to create a range of information skills learning objects that can be embedded into course content across all departments, though there is a realization that the scale of this and the metadata creation associated with it may well have been underestimated!

The librarianship literature includes descriptions of other delivery mechanisms for information skills in contrast to the embedding method, in particular the creation of a credit-bearing 'stand-alone' course by Johnston and Webber (2003). All are valid approaches, the most important thing being that they 'deliver the goods' and work well within the operational environment. An approach in one institution cannot necessarily be replicated in another unless the political, eco-nomic, organizational and pedagogical philosophies are identical. In looking to the future, to the 'transformed library' as Brewer et al. (2004) have done, it is important that 'information fluency is co-owned by the entire campus. Librarians [will] spend less time in front of classes, and more time partnering in curricular and instructional design, and in the assessment of learning.'

New Partnership

New Partnership is the name we have given to the initiative to re-invigorate the dialogue between the Library and academic departments in support of learning and teaching across the University. It represents exactly what we are attempting to encompass through a multi-faceted approach to this support: it does not promote solely e-literacy or information skills; it does not promote just the new methods of perceiving resource lists; it does not promote other initiatives such as course packs. The aim is to present a holistic view of information resources and explore ways in which these can best be used – individually or together – to support student learning: it proactively investigates opportunities and develops best practice for specific instances.

But the New Partnership is also more than this. As already noted, the long-standing relationship between Library and departments has been primarily one-to-one: academic liaison librarian to departmental library representative, though this has often developed into one-to-many when discussing, for example, the reading list requirements of different courses with individual academics. Learning from the interviews in the user needs survey, where enthusiasts had developed their own WebCT courses but had sometimes had difficulty in finding continuation funding or further support within their departments for large-scale take-up, the New Partnership is actively seeking to develop departmental or faculty perspectives to information resources. If large-scale ownership and interest can be engendered, the chances of success are improved, even where this falls short of the creation of departmental policies.

The most important factor is the dialogue. If, instead of the librarian being the one promoting information resources, examples of good reading list practice can be expanded across a whole department, promoted by positive feedback from students, a cascading effect will occur from within: academic talking to academic about new library services that support them and their students. Perhaps one measure of success would be eavesdropping on 'water-cooler' discussions about the organization of reading lists and e-literacy skills instead of the departmental promotions round: the librarian as catalyst or sprinkler of magic dust!

To initiate a meaningful dialogue there must be a message and the correct forum chosen for disseminating the message. At Sheffield, a carefully planned approach of a series of faculty forums to which would be invited key faculty and departmental staff with learning and teaching responsibilities, alongside the departmental library representatives, soon broke down to take advantage of 'the moment'. One such forum was held but then, as informal dialogue about developing library services took place with other key academics, so presentations were given to a range of faculty boards, committees and departmental meetings and away days. These have generated substantial interest and enthusiasm among academics at all levels but it is moving to the next stage that is almost more important and time-consuming, on both sides: taking hold of that enthusiasm while it is still there and transferring it into real deliverables. We are talking about a major culture change here, and culture change does not happen overnight. However, the New Partnership has already started to bear fruit, as evidenced in the paper written jointly by an academic and a member of Library staff from Sheffield (Freeman and Parker, 2004).

It was indicated above that the message being transmitted was one of an holistic approach to information resources to support learning and teaching, presenting the key ways in which the Library could work with departments and developing those most appropriate for current needs. If the dialogue occurs in a meaningful way, other opportunities, perhaps difficult to integrate into the curriculum immediately, can be more widely discussed and developed, and integrated further down the line.

The holistic message emphasizes the adaptability of resource lists and the importance of e-literacy and information skills but doesn't rank one over the other: they are interlinked but not presented as an item on a fast-food menu that can only be delivered in a single, unalterable way. The key message is that this is an adaptable system that enables information resources to be provided in a way that best supports first year students in adapting to the new perspectives and skills required at university, that can be adapted to encourage focused resource discovery as confidence is gained and educational demands increase, and that can be supported by an e-literacy and information skills resource at all times. The student is not left to flounder through a morass of indigestible global resource discovery but can be directed to appropriate readings in a way that supports different pedagogical approaches and without accusations of spoon-feeding (Stubley, 2002).

The message given to departments emphasizes two further advantages from the New Partnership approach: improved resource management; and the promotion of research-led teaching. In common with most academic libraries, the University of Sheffield's journals budget is substantial and, particularly as a result of publishers 'basket deals', the number of full-text titles is ever-increasing (around 6000 in 2004). This extensive and expensive resource is perceived primarily as supporting the University's major research effort but, through the new technology of linked resource lists, it can be seen as a previously untapped resource with which to support the undergraduate curriculum. This may not result in immediate cost savings but, over a period of time, it may change the balance between paper and electronic readings for undergraduates and should lead to a more effective overall use of library resources.

Research-led teaching is a particular feature of universities such as Sheffield with research being introduced into the undergraduate curriculum in a number of ways depending on the focus of individual departments. The resource list approach, allied to the extensive e-journal collection, offers yet another way by which the Library can positively support the aims of the institution and departments while providing better services to students.

Finally, in developing a more proactive dialogue with academic departments, a library might wish to consider whether its internal systems, its organizational structures and, indeed, its staff, can deliver what is required. At Sheffield a review resulted in a reorganization and the creation of an Academic Services Group with the specific remit of supporting not only learning and teaching but also research activity in departments. Using the New Partnership as the compass, we hope that the Library will not in the future be caught in an unexpected predicament and will continue of offer quality services to all of its user population.

References

Bennett, N., Dunne, E. and Carré, C. (1999) Patterns of Core and Generic Skill Provision in Higher Education, *Higher Education*, **37**, 71–93.

Boyd, W. E., Cullen, M., Bass, D., Pittman, J. and Regan, J. (1998) A Response to Apparently Low Levels of Numeracy and Literacy Amongst First Year University Environmental Science Students: a numeracy and literacy skills survey, *International Research in Geographical and Environmental Education*, **7** (2), 106–21.

Boyle, T. (2003) Design Principles for Authoring Dynamic, Reusable Learning Objects, *Australian Journal of Educational Technology*, **19** (1), 46–58.

Brewer, J. M., Hook, S. J., Simmons-Welburn, J. and Williams, K. (2004) Libraries Dealing with the Future Now, *ARL Bimonthly Report*, (June), **234**, www.arl.org/newsltr/234/dealing.html [accessed June 2004].

Corrall, S. and Hathaway, H. (eds) (2000) *Seven Pillars of Wisdom? Good practice in information skills development. Proceedings of a conference held at the University of Warwick, 6–7 July*, London, SCONUL.

Cottrell, S. (1999) *The Study Skills Handbook*, Basingstoke, Macmillan.

Deighton, L. (1965) *Horse Under Water*, Penguin Books, 7. The quotation is from Callingham, *Seamanship: jottings for the young sailor*.

Dillon, C., Needham, G., Hodgkinson, L., Parker, J.and Baker, K. (2003) Information Literacy at the Open University: a developmental approach. In Martin, A. and Rader, H., *Information and IT Literacy: enabling learning in the 21st century*, London, Facet Publishing, 66–76.

Drew, S., Shaw, M. and Mowthorpe, D. (2000) *Key to Key Skills; final report 1, May 2000*, www.shu.ac.uk/keytokey/finalrep4.pdf [accessed June 2004].

Farber, E. (1999) Faculty-librarian Cooperation: a personal retrospective, *Reference Services Review*, **27** (3), 229–234.

File, J. (1984) Student Learning Difficulties and Teaching Methods, *Studies in Higher Education*, **9** (2), 191–4.

Freeman, M. and Parker, L. (2004) Blended learning: blended resources – a collaborative approach to supporting students. In *Networked Learning 2004: proceedings of the fourth annual conference held at Lancaster University, 5–7 April*. University of Sheffield/Lancaster University, 596–601.

Godwin, P. (2003) Information Literacy, But at What Level? In Martin, A. and Rader, H., *Information and IT Literacy: enabling learning in the 21st century*, London, Facet Publishing, 88–97.

Hardesty, L. (1999) Reflections on 25 Years of Library Instruction: have we made progress? *Reference Services Review*, **27** (3), 242–6.

Heseltine, R. (2000) Developing Information Skills for Students: whose responsibility? Academics? In Corrall, S. and Hathaway, H. (eds) (2000) *Seven Pillars of Wisdom? Good practice in information skills development. Proceedings of a conference held at the University of Warwick, 6–7 July*, London, SCONUL, 74–7.

Jenkins, A., Breen, R. and Lindsay, R. (2003) *Reshaping Teaching in Higher Education*, Kogan Page.

Johnson, H. (2003) The SCONUL Task Force on Information Skills. In Martin, A. and Rader, H., *Information and IT*

Literacy: enabling learning in the 21st century, London, Facet Publishing, 45–51.

Johnston, B. and Webber, S. (2003) Information Literacy in Higher Education: a review and case study, *Studies in Higher Education*, **28** (3), 335–52.

Kneale, P. (1997) The Rise of the 'Strategic Student': how can we adapt to cope? In Armstrong, S., Thompson, G. and Brown, S. (eds), *Facing Up To Radical Change in Universities and Colleges*, London, Kogan Page.

Lizzio, A. and Wilson, K. (2004) First-year Students' Perceptions of Capability, *Studies in Higher Education*, **29** (1), 109–28.

Martin, A. (2003) Towards e-literacy. In Martin, A. and Rader, H., *Information and IT Literacy: enabling learning in the 21st century*, London, Facet Publishing, 4–23.

Martin, A. and Rader, H. (2003) *Information and IT Literacy: enabling learning in the 21st century*, London, Facet Publishing.

McAvinia, C. and Oliver, M. (2002) 'But My Subject's Different': a web-based approach to supporting disciplinary lifelong learning skills, *Computers & Education*, **38**, 209–20.

McGuinness, C. (2003) Attitudes of Academics to the Library's Role in Information Literacy Education. In Martin, A. and Rader, H., *Information and IT Literacy: enabling learning in the 21st century*, Facet Publishing, 244–54.

National Committee of Inquiry into Higher Education (1997) *Higher Education in the Learning Society (the Dearing Report), Report 3: Academic staff in Higher Education: their experiences and expectations*, www.leeds.ac.uk/educol/ncihe [accessed June 2004].

Northedge, A. (1990) *The Good Study Guide*, Milton Keynes, Open University.

OCLC E-learning Task Force (2003) *Libraries and the Enhancement of E-learning*, OCLC, 19pp, www.oclc.org/index/elearning/default.htm [accessed June 2004].

Powis, C. (2000) Developing Information Skills for Students: whose responsibility? Plenary discussion. In Corrall, S. and Hathaway, H. (eds) (2000) *Seven Pillars of Wisdom? Good practice in information skills development. Proceedings of a conference held at the University of Warwick, 6–7 July*, London, SCONUL, 78–9.

Race, P. (1999) *How to Get a Good Degree: making the most of your time at university*, Milton Keynes, Open University.

Rowntree, D. (1998) *Learn How to Study: a realistic approach*, London, Warner Books.

Stubley, P. (2002) Going Beyond Resource Discovery, *Library and Information Update*, 1 (6), 52–4.

Sutherland, P. (2003) Case Studies of the Learning and Study Skills of First Year Students, *Research in Post-Compulsory Education*, 8 (3), 425–40.

Town, J. S. (2003) Information Literacy: definition, measurement, impact. In Martin, A. and Rader, H., *Information and IT Literacy: enabling learning in the 21st century*, London, Facet Publishing, 53–65.

Webber, S. and Johnston, B. (2003) Assessment for Information Literacy: vision and reality. In Martin, A. and Rader, H., *Information and IT Literacy: enabling learning in the 21st century*, London, Facet Publishing, 101–11.

Winn, S. (2002) Student Motivation: a socio-economic perspective, *Studies in Higher Education*, 27 (4), 445–57.

6

Collection management

Frances Hall and Jill Lambert

Introduction

Collection management has been summarized as being the 'systematic management of the planning, composition, funding, evaluation and use of library collections' (Cogswell, quoted in Jenkins and Morley, 1999, 2). In this chapter, we will be considering collection management from the perspective of support for e-learning. Specifically, the chapter will consider electronic resources: their selection and funding, and how they are made accessible to users, monitored, licensed, archived and promoted.

As librarians to an increasingly web-based clientele, we need to ask ourselves what constitutes the collection that we are managing? E-learning resources can span a range of material, from traditional resources such as bibliographic databases to emerging media types such as electronic books and multimedia web resources. However, in the electronic arena, the difference between previously well defined categories becomes increasingly blurred. Although we can talk about books, journals and full-text or bibliographic databases, the difference between them may be fluid. On one level, the distinction between the full-text database and bibliographic database is confused by the fact that a database may be partly full-text and partly bibliographic. On another level, there is similar ambiguity between full-text databases and electronic journals.

Library collections in support of e-learning may go beyond familiar categories such as books, journals and databases to encompass datasets, audiovisual clips, image libraries and so on. It is beyond the scope of this chapter to discuss these wider resources in depth. However, decisions may need to be made about just what constitutes a 'library resource' and where the boundaries of the library's responsibility lie.

Although the traditional labels and divisions of a library's collection are becoming blurred, collection management remains just as necessary for e-learners as for more traditional learners. E-learners face particular challenges in their reliance on electronic resources (such as the quantity and poor quality of many free websites), and so it is essential to keep the library at the centre of their learning experience. It has been widely noted that students 'have begun to ignore the library and go directly to the web for their information needs' (OCLC, 2003, 6). The JISC-funded JUBILEE project likewise found a 'heavy, or even complete, reliance on Internet search engines' among staff and students (Coulson, Ray and Banwell, 2003, 440).

Libraries face real competition in providing students with information, especially when speed and ease outweigh quality: see, for example, Markland and Kemp's discovery that the main reasons given for using the internet 'were not good academic ones. These were the speed with which information could be retrieved, and the convenience of working in this way' (Markland and Kemp, 2004, 235). Users have become accustomed to desktop access, to the point where some students are surprised when books and journals which they find via search engines are *not* available to download. Consequently, a balanced, accessible and high-quality collection of electronic resources is essential to maintaining the quality of an e-learner's studies. Indeed, advice to library staff repeatedly emphasizes the importance of e-learners having 'information provision comparable in level and richness to that offered to campus-based students' (SCONUL, 2004, 5).

Resource selection

Electronic journals

For libraries, the acquisition of e-resources requires re-thinking the collection development process. As Montgomery and King (2002) have observed, the selection and acquisition of an electronic collection is far more complex than developing print collections. There are several reasons for this, including changes in the way publishers are selling their information, the fact that resources are usually leased rather than purchased outright and the IT requirements relating to access. With print journals, the practicalities involved in selection are relatively straightforward, with the criteria including academic interest, cost, collection balance, availability in other accessible libraries, quality and levels of usage at the renewal stage. Journals are sold at a standard price and usually ordered from a subscription agent.

These criteria are still essential for the electronic collection but additional factors also come into play. The design of the interface, availability of usage statistics and linking facilities all need consideration, but the overriding factors to consider are the archiving policy, the length of back files and the access rights. The facility to use a journal off-campus, authenticated by a username and password, is an important factor. So too is the facility for many users to search a title simultaneously. Any restrictions about off-campus use or the number of simultaneous accesses can create problems.

Archival policies in particular merit careful consideration when electronic subscriptions are being substituted for print. With many publishers offering discounts for electronic only access, there would seem to be little need to maintain dual print and electronic subscriptions. However, although publishers' licences for electronic journals generally include an archival policy, this may not offer the water-tight security that some libraries need, as discussed further in this chapter. There may also be scenarios where the content remains better suited to print. In the US, Drexel University for instance has migrated to electronic only journals, aside from a minority of cases where electronic subscriptions were not an adequate replacement for print (Montgomery and King, 2002).

Publishers' deals

Described by Frazier (2001) as the 'Librarians' Dilemma', the 'bundles' or deals offered by publishers offer a single price to buy all of a publisher's journals (or a subset of those journals) as a package, at a discount on their list price. One of the best known is Elsevier's ScienceDirect (www.sciencedirect.com/), but there are many others.

Bundling enables publishers to sell the weaker with the stronger titles in one transaction, with economies of scale in dealing with orders. For libraries there are benefits too. The number and range of titles is greatly increased, and it is administratively less time-consuming than dealing with a similar number of titles from many different publishers.

However, each bundle that is purchased reduces the room for manoeuvre, as more and more of a library's budget is committed to these deals, often for several years ahead. The result is that libraries are buying both essential and non-essential titles, unable to pick and mix only the most relevant titles. Although individually 'big deals' offer attractive extra content for the additional money, no library could afford to subscribe to them all because of the increased cost and the lack of flexibility. Once deals containing the most essential titles have been selected, choosing from the remaining deals can be difficult, as it involves weighing the merits of different useful, but non-essential, extra journals.

There is also a major concern that libraries, and more widely academic publishing, are becoming more and more dependent on a small number of companies, enabling them to monopolize the market. This leaves libraries in a vulnerable position, as they cannot choose the bundles that offer the best value for money when some academic staff need specific titles regardless of cost. However, package deals can reveal interesting trends over time, as usage expands out to cover titles to which the library never subscribed in print. This makes it difficult to revert back to subscriptions to the original journals, as well as revealing user interests which may not previously have been obvious.

Electronic books

While the selection of e-journals is more complex than acquiring print subscriptions, there is no doubting the fact that users prefer electronic access. The situation with electronic books is more ambiguous. E-books are not always seen as cost-effective in comparison with their print equivalents. However, they become more cost-effective when they include additional features such as cross-searching or interactive support and are also very useful for quick reference purposes.

When selecting e-books, the primary consideration is the content. Are the titles ones likely to be recommended by lecturers? Academics will not base their reading lists on whether a book is available electronically. However, it can be time-consuming to find out whether reading list books are offered via any of the e-book suppliers, and they may simply not be available electronically. E-books collections may also be oriented towards the US market, or may not include the latest front-list titles.

The second point to consider is how e-books will be used. Electronic reference collections offer significant benefits to users compared with print, in particular desktop access and easy, precise searching. Moreover, electronic encyclopaedias or handbooks, available day and night, may help to wean some students away from free web resources to high quality, evaluated information. However, restrictions on printing and downloading, for example restricting printing to one page at a time, may make it difficult for users who prefer to read from printouts. The typical usage restrictions tend to favour quick reference material which can be accommodated through reading on a screen.

Resource funding

The cost of going electronic

The true cost of e-resources is not always apparent to the user and might be seen as cheaper than traditional library materials. Users also do not realize how expensive e-resources are, as the content is easily accessible and free at the point of use (Pinfield, 2001). Although electronic-based information has enormous benefits to learners, it is a fallacy to believe that it offers an immediately cheaper form of provision.

There are several reasons for this:

- *VAT (Value Added Tax)*. While print material is zero rated in the UK, VAT is payable on electronic resources. Some publishers offer discounted rates for electronic journal subscriptions, up to 15% less in some instances. In many instances, though, the discount on an electronic subscription is small or non-existent, meaning that online is effectively more expensive than print even when the list price is similar.
- *Archival access*. Publishers' licences do not usually include any guarantee of free archival access for the years a journal title has been purchased, if an electronic subscription is subsequently cancelled. It is often necessary to continue with the print version as well as providing electronic access, as a safeguard. In some cases, this means double the costs, although where publishers are charging a small amount extra for combined print and online (for instance 20%), it can work out to be barely more expensive than an online subscription once VAT is included.
- *Cancellation clauses*. Most publishers include clauses in deals for electronic journals which restrict the number of print titles that can be cancelled, to ensure expenditure levels are maintained. The level of cancellations permitted varies with each deal but is not usually more than 5% of the total holdings.

Set against these costs are the savings that electronic resources offer, in terms of 'life-cycle' costs. A case study based on Drexel University indicated that electronic journals are more cost-effective if all expenses, in particular storage space, are taken into account (Montgomery and King, 2002). Another study of US academic libraries, which compared the costs of print and electronic journals, concluded that there could be reductions in long term financial commitments (Schonfeld et al., 2004). With electronic journals, there is no need to increase storage space, bind print copies, re-shelve volumes after use, or carry out maintenance such as obtaining missing parts on inter-library loan. However, these cost savings are predicated on a solution to the long term archival issues of electronic journals.

The case study at Drexel University also confirmed that the largest costs by far are for electronic titles subscribed to individually rather than as part of a package deal or an aggregated database such as Lexis-Nexis Executive (http://web.lexis-nexis.com/executive). The 'big deal' is cheaper for cost per journal, though for a large research library it has been demonstrated that if the non-essential titles are eliminated it could be less expensive to buy individual titles. In 2003 Cornell University made the decision to save money by ending its sub-scription to the ScienceDirect journal package, allowing it to cancel its subscription to a large number of less popular Elsevier titles (Cornell University Library, 2003).

The cheapest cost per title can be found in aggregated full-text data-bases such as Lexis-Nexis Executive and ProQuest which give access to journals from a large range of publishers, although in some data-bases without direct title or issue level links. The main downside of aggregated databases can be the lack of stability. Changes in the contracts between the publishers supplying the journals and the aggregator can result in an essential title being removed at short notice.

The bottom line for libraries is that pricing models for e-resources cannot yet be relied upon to be stable. The charging mechanisms used by publishers are complex and varied, particularly for e-journal deals, and often dependent on a formula based on the spending on print journals and size of the institution, with an additional percentage for electronic access. Considerable time and effort is needed to understand the charge and in subsequently checking that it has been applied correctly by the publisher. Publishers and the Joint Information Systems Committee (JISC) are still experimenting with different business models, including e-journal deals based on past usage.

Internal budgeting constraints

Beyond the complexities of pricing models, the structure of a library's internal budget influences the way e-resources are funded. Decisions on e-resources that are narrowly focused on specific subject fields are relatively easy to make. The main issues are whether the content is relevant enough to warrant the cost and whether there are sufficient funds in the budget for the subject to pay for it.

The difficulties arise with large e-journal deals in cross-disciplinary areas, where the cost has to be spread over many different budget codes. Even when the budget is under the total control of the library, there can be problems if all the funds are rigidly allocated to specific subject areas. Calculating how much should be contributed by each subject can be complex and time-consuming.

For libraries operating with devolved budgets, the situation is even more acute. To purchase a large cross-disciplinary package requires consultation and negotiation with many departments. To some the package will be essential, but others may be lukewarm or indifferent. One solution is to establish a development fund to pay for new deals on a trial basis. At the renewal stage, the usage statistics, provided these are available, can be used as a basis for negotiating the allocation of costs between departments.

In such situations, a flexible approach will be needed in dealing with usage statistics, as these are not likely to be broken down to sub-institutional level. One approach is to allocate journal titles to departments according to subject interests. Although this takes no account of the relative importance attached to titles by different departments, if the package is large, the overall balance is likely to be fair.

Access issues

Once suitable resources have been purchased, the next major concern is how to make them as accessible as possible to users. In theory, the growth of e-learning should encourage greater than ever usage of electronic information resources, by bringing them together with lecture notes, exam-papers and other course material, within a single virtual space.

However, although this is the ideal, users can still face a bewildering range of interfaces: different databases, different journal providers, the library catalogue and the library website as well as their virtual learning environment (VLE).

Integration with the VLE

In the ideal scenario, students find relevant information resources integrated into the e-learning module, with the attendant benefits of speed and ease noted by Jenkins (2002, 54) among others. For example, e-learners could view their reading list in their VLE, and click straight through to the full text if available, either via an external site or via a digitized copy on the VLE. Alternatively, they could see suggestions of useful databases to search for further information. There is a spectrum of options, ranging from a basic link out to the library catalogue, through to users being able to search and view databases from within the VLE.

However, a variety of issues may arise as librarians seek to incorporate digital library resources into the VLE. Ownership of the VLE may lie outside the library, with the consequent need to negotiate access and to gain permission to add or update content. Consultation and negotiation with academic colleagues is also of considerable importance, not least because they may choose to display links to free web resources or search engines instead of the library's subscription resources. Adding and updating reading lists and other information resources can be a time-consuming barrier to academic staff. There may also be technical incompatibilities between the VLE and the service providers, or between the VLE and the library management system. In 2003, the state of linking between digital libraries and VLEs was described as 'rudimentary' (McLean and Lynch, 2003), but it is developing rapidly.

To catalogue or not to catalogue?

Faced with an increasingly large electronic collection, libraries also need to decide what (and how much) to catalogue. Bearing in mind the time-consuming nature of cataloguing, should we consider the library catalogue to be 'at the centre of the hybrid or electronic library or is it "just another database"?' (Pinfield, 2001).

The main argument in favour of adding resources such as databases, electronic books and electronic journals to the catalogue is that it helps the library to integrate its print and electronic collections. The library catalogue can then be promoted as a 'one-stop shop', providing access to as much as possible in one place.

The principal argument against this approach is the time-consuming nature of catalogue maintenance, bearing in mind that holdings of electronic journals and books can change at a fast pace. It can also be argued that even if promoted as a 'one-stop shop', the catalogue will never be a comprehensive place to search, as it does not allow full-text or article level searching. Many users already seem to have difficulty with the notion of searching for journal titles on the OPAC. On balance, the authors favour inclusion of e-resources in the catalogue. Although checking and updating links can be time-consuming, publishers are also increasingly producing stable, title-level URLs for e-journals, reducing the risk of constant changes and out-of-date catalogue records.

Serials management

Initially, many universities made use of static web pages listing their available e-journals. However, as the number of titles increased, and maintenance of such lists took more time, they have increasingly looked towards alternatives. One solution is the development of a home-grown database to contain information about all e-journals and, for example, dynamically generate web page listings. If e-journals are also included on the catalogue, for the reasons already discussed, then a decision needs to be made about whether separate listings of electronic journals can be justified.

Whether it is the catalogue or a separate database which is maintained, there remain a number of potential challenges with e-journals management:

- Holdings of the different aggregators and e-journal collections may change rapidly, and not always with advance notification. As the number of titles increases, it becomes harder to keep track of all available journal subscriptions.
- Access can be time-consuming to set up and maintain, as different publishers have different procedures and requirements, and subscription information may not be correctly passed between library, serials vendor (if there is one) and publisher.
- There may be technical problems, for example with missing content.
- The same journals may be available from more than one source, sometimes with different back-files.

E-journal gateways, such as Swetswise (www.swetswise.com/), TDNet (www.tdnet.com/) and Serials Solutions (www.serialssolutions.com/), have been introduced to help libraries manage these problems. Gateways set up access to subscriptions on the library's behalf and authenticate user access via a single route. They also allow users to search and retrieve content from a range of e-journal publishers via a single interface. As additional advantages, they may undertake automatic link-checking, and provide A–Z and subject-based lists of journal titles.

There are still some potential limitations, namely:

- Not all e-journal gateways will have an agreement for all content, so not all journals will be available for article level searching. For some journals, users must be redirected to another site to access articles.
- Gateways may not have access to the full back-files of journals.
- Uploading the library's journal holdings and keeping them up to date can still be a continuous task.
- Library staff still need to troubleshoot instances where access fails to work, and technical problems with the gateway or the publisher can still occur.

Nonetheless, in spite of these issues, many libraries have opted to make use of an e-journals gateway as the best solution currently available to them. At their best, gateways genuinely make it easier for learners by bringing e-journal provision into one place and allowing it to be kept up to date.

Authentication

Writers on e-learning emphasize the value of integration and 'seamless and transparent services' (Core, Rothery and Walton, 2003, 6). However, e-learners may still be asked to log onto the university network (if on-campus), the VLE, electronic resources (which may or may not be Athens-authenticated) as well as their library borrower accounts. Developments such as Shibboleth (http://shibboleth. internet2.edu/) are beginning to provide international open standards, which should gradually integrate local and external authentication systems and take the onus from the user to keep track of numerous different accounts and logins. Nonetheless, as long as they face multiple logins, authentication remains one of the most confusing issues for end-users.

IP-based access provides an alternative approach, although this does present potential difficulties to off-campus learners, who may need to use dial-in or proxy servers. Where IP access is offered, some features may not be available unless there is also an option for a personal login. The ACM Digital Library (www.acm.org/dl/), for example, has the option to save articles to a personal binder but this is only available to personal subscribers, not to institutions who share one IP-based account.

Reference linking

One possible barrier to users of e-resources is the presentation of material for which the user has no rights of access. Some databases allow subscribed and non-subscribed content to be searched together (such as IEEE Xplore, www.ieee.org/ieeexplore/, which does not allow searches to be restricted to subscription material only). Moreover, even free resources such as web search engines may provide links to subscription-only resources.

This blurring of the boundaries between subscribed and unsubscribed resources makes it difficult for users to differentiate between what should and should not be accessible. The CrossRef initiative, for example, uses Digital Object Identifiers to identify objects such as journal articles uniquely, and associate them with a persistent link to their location on the Internet. With the growth of CrossRef (www.crossref.org/) and other linking initiatives, bibliographic databases increasingly allow users to click on full-text links, to go to an electronic copy of the article if available.

Such full-text links can become misleading as they are not sensitive to the user's context and may offer an inappropriate copy (for example a copy on the publishers website, whereas the user needs to access their library's subscription via an aggregator such as ProQuest). In addition, not all publishers or database providers may be part of agreements such as CrossRef and the links do not cover the complete library collection, such as the print journals.

OpenURL technology offer one possible solution to these difficulties because, unlike CrossRef and similar initiatives, it allows context-sensitive linking. An OpenURL is a URL that contains bibliographic information, such as title, author and volume, in a standard format. An OpenURL-compliant database sends information about an item, in the form of an OpenURL, to the 'resolver'. The resolver then gives the user a range of context-sensitive links, appropriate to that particular user.

Not only can an OpenURL resolver offer the most appropriate copy (links to the electronic full-text with the appropriate publisher, or links to the library catalogue for print journals), it can also offer extended services (for example, search for a book's details on Amazon, or search for the author of an article on Google). It is worth noting that this approach requires the library to maintain a 'knowledge base' of the resolver – tables which note what journal subscriptions are held and where, and which subscription is preferred.

There are some potential problems with OpenURL services. In particular:

- The knowledge base depends on the information provided by vendors about the content of their journal packages, which may not always be accurate.
- The knowledge base also has to be able to cope with split runs, and moving walls (for example when only the last ten years are available).
- Not all databases are OpenURL compliant.

OpenURL technology may raise user expectations too high. There will always be cases where linking does not work, or where the article may simply not be available.

A number of commercial resolvers are available, and EDINA and MIMAS have both implemented open access resolvers (BALSA, http://edina.ac.uk/balsa/, and LitLink, http://litlink.mimas.ac.uk, respectively). If the institution does not have its own resolver, LitLink or BALSA can link users to standard targets such as COPAC or the major journal publishers, although access cannot be guaranteed as it still depends on the individual's institutional subscriptions.

Monitoring usage

Usage of electronic collections is an important factor in renewal decisions, as well as decisions about the amount of promotional effort needed. The Evalued project found that vendor-provided statistics are still the main source of evaluation for most libraries (Thebridge and Hartland-Fox, 2002, 38). However, vendor-supplied reports are notoriously inconsistent in the level of detail and range of usage measures they supply. Possible complications include the fact that IP access and username and password access may generate two sets of statistics; usage reports may cover only the whole database and not break down to the constituent parts (such as individual journal titles); and most usage reports do not allow analysis by subsets of users. Even now, some services, such as the New Scientist Archive, offer no usage figures at all to their institutional subscribers.

Usage reports may include different measures such as the number of searches, viewed results, downloads or turnaways. However, the same term can be described differently by different vendors (Do viewed results include abstracts or only full-text? Do double clicks count as separate requests?). In this environment, the COUNTER initiative is aiming to standardize usage reports, and produced version one of a voluntary code of practice in 2002. The COUNTER code focuses on journals and databases, but electronic books will be covered by a separate code. COUNTER aims to facilitate 'the recording, exchange and interpretation of online usage data' that is 'consistent, credible and compatible' (COUNTER, 2004). It has received the support of a number of major publishers and organizations such as the Association of Research Libraries, whose own E-Metrics project (www.arl.org/stats/newmeas/emetrics/) has also studied the collection and use of data on electronic resources. The work of COUNTER should eventually allow libraries, for example, to aggregate all usage figures for a particular journal, whether users access it via the publisher's website or via e-journals gateway or aggregator (such as Swetswise or ProQuest).

Licensing and copyright

Licences to electronic resources are increasingly being negotiated at a national level. JISC Collections (www.jisc.ac.uk/index.cfm?name= coll), NESLI (www.nesli2.ac.uk) and Eduserv Chest (www.eduserv.org. uk/chest/) all offer longstanding deals to a range of resources, and there can be some security in deals negotiated at this level, in terms of the use of model licences and pre-agreed price increases. However, model licences are only still a proportion of the total licences available, and libraries may be in a more vulnerable position than publishers, many of which have specialist lawyers. At many higher education institutions (HEIs), librarians without specialist knowledge are dealing with licensing issues.

Electronic materials such as electronic journals and books are covered by the same copyright conditions as their print counterparts, including provision for fair dealing by users (Norman, 1999, 45). However, unlike most print materials, electronic resources are governed by licence agreements, and as Pinfield (2001) has commented, these 'private arrangements . . . place the provider in a much stronger position to specify how the information is used and who uses it', compared with public law. Copyright owners are sensitive to protecting their assets in the digital world, where there is the potential for unlimited perfect copying and so will bar or restrict usage which they feel to be excessive. Although in theory licence agreements could allow rights beyond those provided in copyright law, in practice many licences seek to limit copying.

Licences may also restrict walk-in usage, reducing the ability of any students, whether full-time, part-time or distance, to draw on the resources of other university libraries. Even where the database providers allow some walk-in use, the security controls on PC networks are a significant barrier against e-learners who wish to make use of their nearest physical library to enhance their learning. Unless schemes like UK Computing Plus (www.uklibrariesplus.ac.uk/ukcp/) expand, learners will be more tied to the resources of their home institution in the electronic world than they ever were in the world of print.

Users' attention needs to be drawn to relevant terms and conditions of access. There is low awareness of copyright issues on the web even now, with one study, for example, finding that 'None [of the lecturers interviewed] seemed aware that copyright law applied to web-based materials as well as to print-based' (Markland and Kemp, 2004, 234). The Copyright Licensing Agency (CLA) licences allow copying for classroom and course packs in HEIs, but only cover print copying. Copying or scanning of content for use in a VLE is not covered by the CLA licence and needs to be cleared with the copyright holder.

HERON (www.heron.ac.uk) is one possible solution, which offers a national copyright clearance and digitization service, although HEIs must pay an institutional subscription fee before being entitled to use the service. Material ordered through HERON is still subject to copyright clearance fees, which are typically charged on a 'per student per page' basis for the students taking a particular course, although they may also be flat-rate fees.

Alternatively, universities can digitize their own material, under the auspices of the CLA's Higher Education Digitization Licensing Scheme. Each extract still needs to be cleared through the CLA Rapid Clearance Service and fees paid to the copyright owner, either based on a 'per student per page' model (more common if it is recommended reading material) or flat-rate price.

Digitization is an expensive and time-consuming business, and so there may need to be a balance between allocating effort to specific electronic readings or electronic study packs, which may only be usable for a specific length of time by a particular cohort of students, against effort spent on developing wide-ranging collections to encourage independent research.

Access to archives

Preservation and archival access has been recognized as a national issue, for example in a recent call for a 'coordinating archiving service for the UK' (Jones, 2003, 3). Nonetheless, library collection management is slowly shifting emphasis from permanent collections to subscriptions reflecting current interests, 'from managing the physical ownership of resources to managing access to shared digital resources' (Pinfield, 2001).

The emphasis that a library places on archival issues will depend on factors such as the subject area and the attitudes of the users. In fast moving subjects such as computing, where older issues of journals quickly lose their value, and where the expectation of desktop access is very high, archives are less of a concern than they are in subjects where older material is more substantially used. Another question is how core the journals are perceived to be. Journals seen as essential are less likely to be cancelled in the first place, but if they *were* cancelled, it would be more important than ever to have ongoing access to the back-files.

Additionally, there is the question of whether the library sees itself as having a long-term archival role (where paper is still the most reliable solution), or whether it emphasizes being able to provide access to material when and where it is needed. Even if an individual library decides that it cannot take responsibility for long-term preservation, there is still the issue of value for money and users not having access to something for which the institution has already paid.

Although the model NESLI2 licence includes clauses requiring provision for archival access, some publishers are moving away from this. The latest licence for the ACM Digital Library, for example, makes no provision for archival access should individual members of the consortium cancel (although should the whole consortium cancel, an archive would be provided to the consortium as a group).

Promotion

The EDNER (Evaluating the Distributed National Electronic Resource) project found that students' first course of action in researching a topic is often to use internet search engines. Students locate sites that are 'satisficing', defined as resources that are easily found but are not comprehensive and of dubious quality (Brophy, 2002). Academic staff can also be unaware of their library's electronic services (Coulson, Ray and Banwell, 2003). A survey of teaching staff at Manchester Metropolitan University found that they associated 'online' with free websites, and that they had not looked at ways of integrating links to full-text journal articles. The study found that students were mainly provided with either a 'high level icon to the Library web page, or at best a pointer to the appropriate Subject Resources section' within the VLE (Markland and Kemp, 2004, 234).

This lack of awareness might be ascribed to a library's failure to promote its services effectively. It is important that promotion should not be aimed solely at students. Referral by academics is a key factor in encouraging students to use resources.

There are now many routes to information, all competing for users' attention: VLEs, lecturers' websites, commercial services such as Google, as well as libraries and their websites (Rowley, 2003, 19). With so many other pathways, how should libraries encourage the use of their e-resources? The answer is to take the content to the user in whichever way this can be achieved, whether through publicity, training in information literacy or via integration with VLEs or portals used by students.

Stimulated by the need to market their services, academic libraries are using a wide range of methods, including e-mail announcements, vendor demonstrations, articles in campus publications, leaflets, posters and 'how to use' type guides. It is also vital to establish the prominence of the library's website as a gateway to services. Some of these methods, such as posters, could be described as passive compared with demonstrations by vendors, for example. The point is to maintain an ongoing, proactive approach to promotion via a mixture of methods.

Awareness of electronic resources is becoming an established component of information literacy programmes. As the range and type of e-resources becomes more complex, the need to equip students with skills to navigate databases and evaluate information has become even more significant. A SCONUL briefing paper covering information support for e-learning suggested that information literacy training should be an integral part of the learning outcomes of the course (SCONUL, 2004, 5). Embedding training within courses was also supported by an OCLC Task Force, which explored the issues associated with academic libraries and e-learning (OCLC, 2003, 14).

Support and training is time-consuming, however. Montgomery and King (2002) found that the staff costs of helping users with electronic journals collection at Drexel University was more than three times that for answering questions related to print titles. The OCLC Task Force also highlighted the challenges that libraries face in providing appropriate training that is also scalable. It suggested the goal of 'just-enough-just-in-time-just-for-me' as an objective, with the construction of generic and specific training modules which could be embedded as learning objects in courses (OCLC, 2003, 14).

While conventional methods of training (such as lectures, hands-on workshops and face-to-face help via enquiry points) still predominate, developments in electronic database tutorials are underway. The INHALE project (http://inhale.hud.ac.uk) at Huddersfield University developed a set of web-based information skills units, some 'free-standing', and some which could be embedded within a Blackboard VLE. These tutorials have subsequently been scaled up and tested by Loughborough and Oxford University Libraries in the INFORMS project (www.lboro.ac.uk/library/INFORMS.html). The results proved that electronic tutorials can be successfully used as an alternative training mechanism and are effective in raising awareness by students of good quality information resources.

Locally produced material

As well as commercial resources, collection management is beginning to involve locally produced resources. Typically such resources might include examination papers, student projects, book chapters or images taken from the library's special collections.

All of these kinds of locally digitized materials can be put up on VLEs (copyright permitting), as resources for e-learners to use. E-learning need not simply mean having access to electronic versions of existing teaching materials. As VLEs progress beyond the role of document repository, a greater range of learning objects will inevitably be produced, in the form of interactive simulations, quizzes, audio-visual clips and so on.

A learning object can be defined as 'any entity . . . which can be used, re-used or referenced during technology supported learning' (Dolphin and Miller, 2002). As has been noted, learning objects are time-consuming to produce (Dolphin and Miller, 2002; Littlejohn and Buckingham Shum, 2003, 1), but one of their key benefits is the potential for re-use. This 'flexibility of content' has been promoted by Charles Clarke, as Secretary of State for Education and Skills, as one of the primary benefits of ICT (JISC, 2003, 7).

Accordingly, universities are being urged to develop ways of sharing learning objects, and libraries, thanks to their experience in information storage and retrieval, are being encouraged to become involved (OCLC, 2003). The guide to e-learning for support staff of the Learning and Teaching Support Network (LTSN) recommends that 'Every university would be wise to develop an institution-wise system for storing or locating digital resources and indeed a method of classifying and finding them once stored' (Core, Rothery and Walton, 2003, 16).

Objects must be found before they can be successfully re-used, and so metadata is an important consideration. Like the catalogue record, which allows users to find a library book, the metadata record allows users to locate and potentially re-use learning objects. It could include a description of who created it, when it was created and so on, as well as information about the pedagogical context (at what level of ability is it aimed, for example). There are a number of standards available: Dublin Core (http://dublincore.org/), IEEE Standard for Learning Object Metadata (http://ltsc.ieee.org/wg12/index.html) and IMS Learning Resource Metadata (www.imsglobal.org/metadata/) are three of the most common.

Once a metadata standard has been agreed upon, compatibility issues need to be addressed, such as the need for controlled vocabulary or a classification system to make the metadata records possible to search usefully. Learning objects are generally created and controlled outside of the library, with little awareness, on the part of those creating the learning object, of the relevant skills held by library staff. Some work has yet to be done in overcoming such barriers, so that libraries are able to add learning objects to their collection strategies. First, it is necessary for those creating learning objects to recognize the concept of sharing and re-use; secondly, library and information professionals need to share their experience in aggregating content and creating metadata.

There are some examples of working learning object repositories which give an idea of what is possible. MERLOT (Multimedia Educational Resource for Learning and Online Teaching) is a US site at www.merlot.org/, which provides a database of peer-reviewed learning materials managed by a consortium of US HEIs. UK Engineering resources can be found at http://searchlt.engineering.ac.uk/.

Future developments

Along with the trend for increasing use of the web in teaching, the balance of library collections is slowly but surely moving from print to electronic, particularly with journals and reference books, and more slowly with textbooks. Access is improving as new standards for authentication and linking are established, and as library management system suppliers develop new tools for interfacing with electronic resources and VLEs.

In the past, 'collection' typically implied long-term physical ownership. However, users' immediate needs are for fast, easy electronic access, and so libraries are increasingly opting for arrangements which are inevitably more short term. Since electronic resources are usually leased rather than purchased, there is always a risk of losing the resource in future if funds do not continue to be available, and even if resources are purchased outright there is the risk of technical obsolescence. Nonetheless, the short-term gains are substantial, in terms of popularity with users and maintaining the library's role as a reference resource against the competition of internet search engines. Consequently, for many, the longer-term risks are worth taking.

This does mean that libraries are rethinking their collection development policies, whether this is explicitly stated or not, to consider how to balance short-term gains versus long-term security. The main danger is that decisions may be made in a piecemeal way, which is why Lee urges his readers that 'libraries should formulate an overall "coherent" collection development policy covering all material' (2004, 9).

However, a SCONUL report has noted that 'replicating the richness and depth of even the less well-founded academic libraries in virtual form is currently an impossibility in most disciplines' (SCONUL, quoted in Johnston, 2001). Interestingly, a JISC project in 2003 investigating the use of VLEs in a new medical school found that students with a less adequate library provision did not use the VLE more to compensate and that 'staff and students want to be able to access both digital and hardcopies' (McLachlan et al., 2003, 9). It follows that e-learners need a blended approach to their use of both the virtual and the physical library. In a majority of institutions, e-learning is being combined with a range of more traditional teaching methods, and similarly in libraries there is unlikely to be an immediate shift towards purely electronic services. The hybrid library, neither fully print nor fully electronic, therefore remains central to the support of e-learners.

References

Brophy, P. (2002) Evaluating the Distributed National Electronic Resource: the EDNER Project, *Vine*, **32** (11), 7–11.

Core, J., Rothery, A. and Walton, G. (2003) *A Guide for Support Staff*, Learning and Teaching Support Network, Generic Centre e-Learning Series no. 5, York, LTSN, www.ltsn.ac.uk/application.asp?app=resources.asp&process =full_record&section=generic&id=325/.

Cornell University Library (2003) *Issues in Scholarly Communication: the Elsevier Subscription*, Ithaca NY, Cornell University, www.library.cornell.edu/scholarlycomm/elsevier.html.

Coulson, G., Ray, K, and Banwell, L. (2003) The Need for a Converged Approach to EIS Provision? Evidence from the JUBILEE Project, *Library Review,* **52** (9), 438–43.

COUNTER (2004) *The COUNTER Code of Practice*, Edinburgh, Counting Online Usage of NeTworked Electronic Resources, www.projectcounter.org/code_practice.html.

Dolphin, I. and Miller, P. (2002) Learning Objects and the Information Environment, *Ariadne*, **32**, www.ariadne.ac.uk/issue32/iconex/intro.html.

Frazier, K. (2001) The Librarians' Dilemma: contemplating the costs of the 'Big Deal', *D-Lib Magazine*, **7** (3), www.dlib.org/dlib/march01/frazier/03frazier.html.

Jenkins, C. and Morley, M. (1999) *Collection Management in Academic Libraries*, 2nd edn, Aldershot, Gower Publishing.

Jenkins, R. (2002) Supporting E-learning at the University of Birmingham, *SCONUL Newsletter*, **25**, 53–6.

Johnston, P. (2001) After the Big Bang: forces of change and e-Learning, *Ariadne*, **27**, www.ariadne.ac.uk/issue27/johnston/intro.html.

Joint Information Systems Committee (2003) The Future of E-Learning, *JISC inform*, (Autumn), 5–7.

Jones, M. (2003) *Archiving E-Journals Consultancy – Final Report.* London, Joint Information Systems Committee, www.jisc.ac.uk/uploaded_documents/ejournalsfinal.pdf.

Lee, S. D. and Boyle, F. (2004) *Building an Electronic Resource Collection: a practical guide*, London, Facet Publishing.

Littlejohn, A. and Buckingham Shum, S. (eds) (2003) Reusing Online Resources, *Journal of Interactive Media in Education* (special issue), 1, www-jime.open.ac.uk/2003/1.

Markland, M. and Kemp, B. (2004) Integrating Digital Resources into Online Learning Environments to Support the Learner. In Banks, S. et al., *Networked Learning 2004: proceedings of the fourth international conference on networked learning 2004, jointly organized by Lancaster University and the University of Sheffield, and held at Lancaster University, Lancaster, 5–7 April 2004*, Lancaster, Lancaster University, www.shef.ac.uk/nlc2004/Proceedings/ProceedingsNL2004.pdf.

McLachlan, J., McHarg, J., Goding, L. and Caldarone, E. (2003), *An Evaluation of the Use of a Virtual Learning Environment and Digital Libraries in a New Medical School: JISC final report*, London, Joint Information Systems Committee, www.jisc.ac.uk/uploaded_documents/divle-pms-final-report.doc.

McLean, N. and Lynch, C. (2003) *Interoperability Between Information and Learning Environments – Bridging the Gaps*, IMS Global Learning Consortium, www.imsglobal.org/DLims_white_paper_publicdraft_1.pdf.

Montgomery, C. H. and King, D. W. (2002) Comparing Library and User Related Costs of Print and Electronic Journal Collections: a first step towards a comprehensive analysis, *D-Lib Magazine*, 8 (10), www.dlib.org/dlib/october02/montgomery/10montgomery.html.

Norman, S. (1999) *Copyright in Further and Higher Education Libraries*, 4th edn, London, Library Association Publishing.

Online Computer Library Center E-Learning Task Force (2003). *Libraries and the Enhancement of E-learning*, Dublin, OH, OCLC, www5.oclc.org/downloads/community/elearning.pdf.

Pinfield, S. (2001) Managing Electronic Library Services: current issues in UK higher education institutions, *Ariadne*, **29**, www.ariadne.ac.uk/issue29/pinfield/intro.html.

Rowley, J. (2003) Information Marketing: seven questions, *Library Management*, **24** (1/2), 13–19.

Schonfield, R. C., King, D. W., Okerson, A. and Fenton, E. G. (2004) Library Periodicals Expenses: comparison of non-subscription costs of print and electronic formats on a life-cycle basis, *D-Lib Magazine*, **10** (1), www.dlib.org/dlib/january04/schonfield/o1schonfield.html.

Society of College, National and University Libraries (2004) *Information Support for eLearning: principles and practice* (revised edition), London, SCONUL, www.sconul.ac.uk/pubs_stats/pubs/info_support_elearning.pdf.

Thebridge, S. and Hartland-Fox, R. (2002) Towards a Toolkit for Evaluating Electronic Information Services, *SCONUL Newsletter*, **27**, 37–43.

Index

academic staff
  relationships, library staff 123–6, 131–4
  skills needs 121–6
access
  authentication 25–6, 150–1
  authorization 25–6
  BALSA 152–3
  cataloguing 148
  collection management 147–53
  COPAC 152–3
  CrossRef 151
  Digital Object Identifiers 151
  digital repositories 23–4
  e-learning systems 20–2
  EDINA 152–3
  electronic journals 147–53
  federated searching 24–5
  IEEE Xplore 151
  integration 147–8
  IP-based 151
  library management system 23
  LitLink 152–3
  management 25–6
  MIMAS 152–3
  OpenURL 152–3
  portals 25
  reference linking 151–3
  resource descriptions 22–3
  resources 20–6
  serials management 149
  technology 29–30
actors, TASCOI component 41
administration streamlining, MLEs 9–10
architectures, MLEs 7

archival access, collection
  management 144, 156
archival policies, electronic
  journals 141–2
Athens database, access 21
authentication, access 25–6, 150–1
awareness, raising 157–8

BALSA, access 152–3
blended learning, SCONUL 73
books, electronic *see* electronic books
budgeting, collection management 146–7
bundling, collection management 142–3
business processes 45–7

cancellation clauses, collection
  management 144
cataloguing, collection management 148
CCNMTL *see* Columbia Center for New
  Media Teaching and Learning
Centre for Educational Technology
  Interoperability Standards (CETIS)
  36–7
CETIS *see* Centre for Educational
  Technology Interoperability
  Standards
change management 55–83
  background 56
  Change Management Toolkit 63–4
  CILIP 63–4
  communities of practice 76–7
  current position 58
  e-learning structures 65–70
  e-learning vision 57

change management (*cont.*)
  EFFECTS 73
  IMPEL2 63–5
  staff development 72–7
  staffing structures 77–9
  strategy development 62–70
  strategy implementation 70–2
  success steps 70–2
  teams, effective 73–6
  VLEs 58–62
  Why Transformation Efforts Fail 70–2
Change Management Toolkit
  CILIP 63–4
  strategy implementation 70–1
changes
  institutional processes 48–9
  need for 40–5
  organizational 48–9
  process of 39–50
  requirements 52
  technological 48–9
Chartered Institute of Library and
  Information Professionals (CILIP),
    Change Management Toolkit 63–4
CLA *see* Copyright Licensing Agency
CMS *see* Course Management System
collaboration
  MLEs 16–19
  teaching departments 16–19
collection management 139–64
  access 147–53
  archival access 144, 156
  budgeting 146–7
  bundling 142–3
  cancellation clauses 144
  cataloguing 148
  copyright 154–5
  Cornell University 145
  cost impact 144–7
  databases 148
  Drexel University 145, 158
  electronic books 143
  electronic journals 141–2
  future developments 160–1
  JISC 146
  licensing 154–5
  locally produced material 159–60
  LTSN 159

  monitoring usage 153–4
  preservation 156
  promotion 157–8
  publishers' deals 142–3
  resource funding 144–7
  resource selection 141–3
  savings 145–6
  SCONUL 161
  scope 139–40
  serials management 149–50
  VAT (Value Added Tax) 144
  VLEs 147–8
Columbia Center for New Media
  Teaching and Learning
    (CCNMTL) 85–111
  see also new media
Columbia University
  CCNMTL 85–111
  CMS 94–7
  VITAL 91–4, 95
commercial VLEs 66
communications, new media 98–103
communities of practice,
  change management 76–7
content packaging, standards 36
contextualised model, embedding skills
  129
COPAC, access 152–3
copyright
  collaboration 17
  collection management 154–5
  electronic journals 154–5
  HERON 155
Copyright Licensing Agency
  (CLA) 155
Cornell University, collection
  management 145
cost impact
  collection management 144–7
  technology 30
COUNTER, monitoring usage 153–4
Course Management System (CMS),
  Columbia University 94–7
CrossRef, access 151
culture of engagement, new media
  98–103
customers, TASCOI component 41

data layer, e-learning structures 69
databases
  Athens 21
  collection management 148
  Lexis-Nexis Executive 145
  ProQuest 145
Dearing Report 116–17
design research process, new
    media 96–7
dialogue, partnerships 131–4
Digital Object Identifiers, access 151
digital repositories, MLEs 23–4
digitization 155
directed model, embedding skills 129
Drexel University
  collection management 145, 158
  electronic journals 141–2
Dublin Core standard 160

E-learning Framework programme
  implications 38–9
  JISC 38–9
e-learning structures
  change management 65–70
  data layer 69
  hardware 69–70
  information resources 68
  layers 66–7
  learning activities 67
  learning components 67–8
  operating system 69
  overseeing the process 70
  planning 66–7
  software layer 68–9
e-learning systems, accessing
    resources 20–2
e-learning vision, change
    management 57
e-literacy
  academic staff 121–6
  embedding resources 115
  skills needs 118–26
  students, 21st century 116–20
  terminology 115–16
  wider perspective 113–37
EDINA, access 152–3
EDNER see Evaluating the Distributed
    National Electronic Resource

Educause Review 110
Effective Framework for Embedding
    C and IT using Targeted Support
    (EFFECTS), change
    management 73
electronic books, collection
    management 143
electronic environment,
    information skills 126–31
electronic journals
  access 147–53
  archival policies 141–2
  budgeting 146–7
  bundling 142–3
  challenges 149–50
  collection management 141–3, 144–61
  copyright 154–5
  gateways 149–50
  licensing 154–5
  ScienceDirect 142, 145
Elsevier, ScienceDirect 142, 145
embedding resources, e-literacy 115
embedding skills 128–31
enterprise, standards 36
ETHICS method, information
    gathering 46–7
Evaluating the Distributed National
    Electronic Resource (EDNER) 157
Exchange for Learning (X4L)
    programme, interoperability 37

FDTL see Fund for the Development of
    Teaching and Learning
federated searching, MLEs 24–5
Free On-line Dictionary of Computing
    (FOLDOC) 66
French, teaching 94–7
Fund for the Development of Teaching
    and Learning (FDTL) 57
funding, collection management 144–7
future developments, collection
    management 160–1

gateways, electronic journals 149–50
Ginsburg, Prof. Herbert 91–4
grants, new media 102
A Guide to Managing Knowledge:
    cultivating communities of practice 76

handbook, new media 105–8
hardware, e-learning structures 69–70
HERON, copyright 155
higher education institutions (HLEs)
    changes 29, 30–1
    operation 29
    organization 29, 30–1
history importance, new media 87–91
HLEs *see* higher education institutions
home grown VLEs 66
Huddersfield University,
        INHALE project 158

identities
    organizational 40–5
    service department 43–5
IEEE Standard for Learning
    Object Metadata 160
IEEE Xplore, access 151
Impact on People of Electronic Libraries
    project (IMPEL2) 63–5
IMS Learning Resource Metadata 160
inertia, universities 51–2
information gathering,
        ETHICS method 46–7
information resources,
        e-learning structures 68
information revolution 3–4
Information Services Change
        Management Programme 75
information skills, electronic
        environment 126–31
*Information Support for E-learning:
    principles and practice* 15–16
INFORMS project, promotion 158
INHALE project, promotion 158
InspireProject 61–2
institutional processes 45–7
    changes 48–9
    problems 45–9
integrated MLEs 14–15, 21–2
University of Ulster 22–3
integrated model, embedding skills 129
integrated user support 9
integration, VLEs 147–8
interfaces, MLEs 6
internet phase, learning technologies 33
internet, reasons for using 140

interoperability
    advantages 37
    CETIS 36–7
    JISC 36–7
    JORUM 37
    MLEs 35–7
    RELOAD 37
    standards 36–7
    TOIA 37
    X4L 37
intervenors, TASCOI component 42
intramural strategic
        relationships, new media 103–5
IP-based access 151

Jackson, Shirley Ann 110
Joint Information Systems
        Committee (JISC)
    collection management 146
    E-learning Framework
        programme 38–9, 56
    interoperability 36–7
    MLEs development 2, 10, 12, 14, 35,
        56
JORUM, interoperability 37
journals, electronic *see*
        electronic journals

layers, e-learning structures 66–7
LDU *see* Learning Development Unit
learner information packaging,
        standards 36
learning activities, e-learning
        structures 67
Learning and Teaching
        Support Network (LTSN),
        collection management 159
learning components,
        e-learning structures 67–8
Learning Development Unit
        (LDU), communities of practice
        76–7
Learning Object Metadata (LOM) 19
learning objects, MLEs 19
learning technologies
    development 31–9
    internet phase 33
    MLEs 35–6

learning technologies (*cont.*)
  multimedia phase 32
  VLE phase 33–4
Lexis-Nexis Executive database 145
Library and Computing Services,
    organizational convergence 63
library and information services (LIS),
    roles 50–1
library management system, MLEs 23
Library Service Point (LSP),
    University of Ulster 21
library staff/academics,
    relationships 123–6, 131–4
licensing
  collection management 154–5
  electronic journals 154–5
LIS *see* library and information services
LitLink, access 152–3
local media, new media 100–1
locally produced material, collection
    management 159–60
LOM *see* Learning Object Metadata
LSP *see* Library Service Point
LTSN *see* Learning and
    Teaching Support Network

managed learning environments
    (MLEs) 1–28
  administration streamlining 9–10
  architectures 7
  collaboration 16–19
  copyright 17
  defining 2
  design 12–14
  development 4–5, 10–16, 35, 56
  digital repositories 23–4
  e-learning support 8
  federated searching 24–5
  implementing 14–16, 35
  integrated 14–15, 21–2
  integrated user support 9
  interfaces 6
  interoperability 35–7
  JISC study 56
  learning objects 19
  learning technologies 35–6
  library management system 23
  metadata 18–19
  models 8–10
  need for 2–4
  objectives 11–12
  organizational perspectives 7
  perspectives 6–7
  priorities 14–16
  questions for consideration 12
  resource management 17–19
  stakeholders, identifying 10–11
  strategic objectives 11–12
  strategy achievement 4–5
  technical view 6–7
  University of Ulster 15
  user support, integrated 9
  vision 14
media, new *see* new media
metadata
  MLEs 18–19, 36
  standards 36, 159–60
MIMAS, access 152–3
MLEs *see* managed learning
    environments
models
  e-learning support 79–80
  embedding skills 128–31
  MLEs 8–10
Monash University 61
monitoring usage
  collection management 153–4
  COUNTER 153–4
multimedia phase, learning
    technologies 32

National Committee of Inquiry into
    Higher Education (NCIHE)
    116–17
national media, new media 101
NCIHE *see* National Committee of
    Inquiry into Higher Education
new media
  CCNMTL 85–111
  communications 98–103
  culture of engagement 98–103
  design research process 96–7
  grants 102
  guide 105–8
  handbook 105–8
  history importance 87–91

new media (*cont.*)
  intramural strategic
    relationships 103–5
  local media 100–1
  national media 101
  organizational website 99–100
  outreach 98–103
  partnerships 103–5
  personal contact 99
  presentations 100
  realpolitik 100
  research/pedagogy tools 102–3
  senior faculty 102
  service organizations 103–5
  sponsoring events 101
  strategic alliances 100
  strategic relationships 103–5
  support 85–111
  vignettes of practice 91–7
  websites 99–100
  workshops 100
New Partnership 131–4

objectives, MLEs 11–12
Online Computer Library
  Center, Inc. (OCLC) 72–3
  promotion 158
Open Archive Initiative 24–5
open source VLEs 66
OpenURL, access 152–3
operating system, e-learning
  structures 69
optional model, embedding
  skills 128–9
organization, HLEs 29, 30–1
organizational identity 40–5
organizational website, new
  media 99–100
outreach, new media 98–103
owners, TASCOI component 41

partnerships
  dialogue 131–4
  new media 103–5
  New Partnership 131–4
  process and 29–53
personal contact, new media 99
personalization of learning 59–60

SCONUL 80–1
planning, e-learning structures 66–7
portals, access 25
presentations, new media 100
preservation, collection management 156
processes
  institutional 45–7, 48–9
  and partnerships 29–53
  problems 45–9
promotion
  collection management 157–8
  EDNER 157
  INFORMS project 158
  INHALE project 158
  OCLC 158
  SCONUL 158
  universities 158
ProQuest database 145
publishers' deals, collection
  management 142–3

quality impact, technology 30
question and test interoperability, standards 36

realpolitik, new media 100
reference linking, access 151–3
relationships
  academics/library staff 123–6, 131–4
  intramural strategic relationships
    103–5
  University of Sheffield 123–6, 131–4
  see also partnerships
RELOAD, interoperability 37
requirements, information
  gathering 46–7
research/pedagogy tools, new
  media 102–3
resource funding, collection
  management 144–7
resource selection
  bundling 142–3
  collection management 141–3
  electronic books 143
  electronic journals 141–2
  publishers' deals 142–3
resources
  access 20–6

resources (*cont.*)
  descriptions 22–3
  embedding 115
  management 17–19
  MLEs 17–19
responsibilities, information
    gathering 46–7
roles, information gathering 46–7

SAKAI project 39
ScienceDirect, Elsevier 142, 145
SCONUL *see* Society of College,
    National and University Libraries
SCORM *see* Sharable Content
    Object Reference Model
senior faculty, new media 102
serials management
  access 149
  challenges 149–50
  collection management 149–50
  see also electronic journals
service department identities 43–5
service organizations, new media 103–5
service-oriented architecture (SOA) 38
Seven Pillars model, SCONUL 113–14
Sharable Content Object Reference
    Model (SCORM) 19
Shibboleth authentication 150
skills
  electronic environment 126–31
  embedding 128–31
  incorporating 128–31
skills needs
  academic staff 121–6
  e-literacy 118–26
  students, 21st century 118–20
Snow Crash 89
SOA *see* service-oriented
    architecture
Society of College, National and
    University Libraries (SCONUL)
  blended learning 73
  collection management 161
  Information Support for E-learning:
    principles and practice 15–16
  personalization of learning 80–1
  promotion 158
  Seven Pillars model 113–14

software layer, e-learning structures
    68–9
sponsoring events, new media 101
staff development, change
    management 72–7
staff relationships, academics
    123–6, 131–4
stakeholders, identifying, MLEs 10–11
standards
  CETIS 36–7
  interoperability 36–7
  metadata 36, 159–60
strategic alliances, new media 100
strategic objectives, MLEs 11–12
strategic questions, VLEs 65–6
strategic relationships, new
    media 103–5
strategy development, change
    management 62–70
strategy implementation, change
    management 70–2
students, 21st century 116–20
  Dearing Report 116–17
  skills needs 118–20
success steps, change management 70–2
suppliers, TASCOI component 41
Swetswise gateway 149–50

TASCOI
  impact 45
  organizational identity 41–5
  responses 43–4
Teaching and Learning Technology
    Programme (TLTP) 32, 57
teaching departments,
    collaboration 16–19
teams, effective
  change management 73–6
  characteristics 74–5
technology
  access 29–30
  availability 49–50
  cost impact 30
  history importance 87–91
  impact 29–30
  see also learning technologies;
    new media
terminology, e-literacy 115–16

TLTP *see* Teaching and Learning
    Technology Programme
TOIA, interoperability 37
transformation, TASCOI component 41
Twigg, Carol 110

UCISA survey (2003) 62
UK Computing Plus 61–2
UK Learning Object Metadata
    (UK LOM Core) 19
UK Libraries Plus 61–2
universities
    Drexel University 141–2, 145, 158
    Huddersfield University 158
    inertia 51–2
    Monash University 61
    promotion 158
University of Birmingham,
    e-learning support 78–9
University of Highlands and
    Islands 60–1
University of Sheffield
    relationships 123–6
    WebCT 123–6, 127–31
University of Ulster
    integrated MLEs 22–3
    LSP 21
    MLEs 15
user support
    integrated 9
    MLEs 9

VAT (Value Added Tax),
    collection management 144
Video Interactions for Teaching
    and Learning (VITAL) 91–4, 95

virtual learning environments (VLEs)
    change management 58–62
    collection management 147–8
    commercial 66
    home grown 66
    impact 34
    Institutional VLEs 59
    integration 147–8
    learning technologies 33–4
    limitations 37
    open source 66
    single vs. range 65–6
    strategic questions 65–6
Vista 130
VITAL *see* Video Interactions
    for Teaching and Learning
VLEs *see* virtual learning
    environments

Web Service Description
    Language (WSDL) 38
WebCT, University of Sheffield
    123–6, 127–31
websites, new media 99–100
Why Transformation Efforts Fail,
    change management 70–2
workshops, new media 100
WSDL *see* Web Service
    Description Language

X4L *see* Exchange for Learning
    programme

Z39.50 protocol, federated
    searching 24